Praise for

WHEN THE CENTURY WAS YOUNG

BY DEE BROWN

"A graceful, warmhearted memoir." —*Publishers Weekly*

"From his small-town Louisiana and Arkansas origins, to his lengthy career as agricultural librarian at the University of Illinois, Brown has seen most of the 20th century, his memories reflecting to a considerable degree the fast changes wrought in America during this time. Throughout his narrative, self-effacement triumphs, [and it is] told easily and with charm."
—*Kirkus Reviews*

"Brown has given us a picture of much more than his own life. He has written a great story that will grab you with its humor and its intensity." —*San Antonio Express-News*

"Brown writes with wit and no airs. Such anecdotes as his encounters with Arkansas hillbillies and his dealings with bureaucracy responsible for classified documents are intelligent slapstick. [Others] may drop tears on the page."
—*The Oklahoman*

ALSO BY DEE BROWN

When The Century Was Young

Dee Brown

HarperPerennial

A Division of HarperCollinsPublishers

Some short segments of this publication appeared in variations in *Growing Up Western*, edited by Clarus Backes (Alfred A. Knopf, 1989), *Contemporary Authors Autobiography Series* (Gale Publishing Company), the *Arkansas Times*, and *Native Arts West*.

This book was originally published in 1993 by August House, Inc. It is here reprinted by arrangement with August House, Inc.

HarperCollins books may be purchased for educational, business, or sales promotional use. For information please write: Special Markets Department, HarperCollins Publishers, Inc., 10 East 53rd Street, New York, NY 10022.

First HarperPerennial edition published 1994.

Library of Congress Cataloging-in-Publication Data

Brown, Dee Alexander.
    When the century was young / Dee Brown. — 1st HarperPerennial ed.
      p.   cm.
    Originally published: Little Rock : August House Publishers, 1993.
    ISBN 0-06-097579-2
    1. Brown, Dee Alexander—Biography. 2. Novelists, American—20th
century—Biography. 3. Historians—United States—Biography. I. Title.
    [PS3503.R79533Z475   1994]
    813´.54—dc20
    [B]   94-12377

94 95 96 97 98 CW 10 9 8 7 6 5 4 3 2 1

In memory of
Robert B. Downs, mentor and friend

Contents

Daniel Alexander Brown, about 1907

CHAPTER ONE

Discovering the World of Print

THE EARLY PART OF THIS CENTURY was the golden age of print, and I was born into it. Newspapers, magazines, and books—in that order—were the major sources of information and entertainment. Radio and television came later as interloping marvels, but even to this day the electronic devices do not match the authority of print.

One of my few memories of my father, Daniel Alexander Brown, who was killed when I was four, is of his reading to me the Sunday comics in the *Shreveport Times* while I sat in his lap looking at the cartoon figures held in front of me. One of the contemporary strips had a character named Buster Brown, and I assumed that Buster was a relative among all the numerous Brown kinfolk in the Bienville Lumber Company's sawmill town of Alberta, Bienville Parish, Louisiana.

The world that I was born into bore little resemblance to the world we live in today. It was so close to the nineteenth century that I have always felt a kinship with that era, which was then very slowly beginning to disappear. I remember these: horse-drawn carriages, button shoes, corsets and feathered hats for women, maypoles in the schoolyards in springtime, quiet orderly schoolrooms, five-cent soda pop and snack foods, mule-drawn wagons and plows, quilting bees, spelling bees, magic lanterns, kinetoscopes, and silent movies. Mark Twain died when I was two, but as a youth I was very much aware of the unseen yet living presences of Buffalo Bill Cody, Thomas Edison, Teddy Roosevelt, President Woodrow Wilson, Henry Ford, Kaiser Wilhelm of Germany, Mrs. George Armstrong Custer, and real cowboys and Indians, including Hollow-Horn Bear, the Sioux chief whose face appeared on a postage stamp after his death.

Included in my natural environment were steam locomotives,

Civil War veterans' reunions, Victorian attitudes, genuine patriotism, baseball players who loved the game as well as money, efficient railroads and trolleys, long flannel underwear, inexpensive books, gadgets that were easily repaired and were usable for years, Model-T Fords, frequent and sudden fatal diseases, depressing funerals held in family parlors, hellfire-and-damnation sermons, religious revivals under big tents, and politicians who apparently believed in honor and country. Some of these things were splendid; others struck terror, especially in the hearts of the young.

I was five when my widowed mother, Lula Cranford Brown, moved us from Louisiana to the town of Stephens in Ouachita County, Arkansas—the southwestern coastal plain, as geographers map that area. We traveled there by railway train, a journey that I but dimly remember. I do recall vividly, however, our arrival at the house where we would live through the next decade into my middle teens. Perhaps the occasion was impressed upon me by the number of adults—my mother's two sisters, their husbands, and others whose identities I do not recall—who met us at the railway station. They made numerous comments about the house and its grounds while we were approaching the place. As the adults and my sister, Corinne, and I came walking up a grassy slope to a wooden gate in a wire fence, we were greeted by a flood of blossoms at our feet, hundreds of bright multicolored phlox in total disorder. Seed had been washed through the fence onto a small sandy-clay delta created by run-off from spring rains. Through the fence we could see similar but not so lush flowers in broken borders on each side of a red-brick sidewalk inside the untended yard.

As we entered through the gate, one of the men—an uncle probably—pointed out a large fig bush far to the right, and a tall chinaberry in the left corner. Both were in full leaf. Then one of my mother's sisters said something about a fire-blackened hollow stump no more than a foot high a few yards to our left. She called attention to the evidences of past attempts to burn and uproot it from the earth. The black stump would play a symbolic role from time to time throughout the years we lived there.

The house had been built and lived in for a short time by relatives—the H.P. Morgans. The wife had recurrent dreams of pots of gold being found under a sweetgum tree in the front yard. The dreams were so vivid that the wife persuaded the husband to cut the tree down and dig under its roots. She had died before all of the stump was burned and removed, although workmen had dug all around it. In his grief the husband refused to continue living in the house and sold it to my mother.

The morning of our arrival we entered the house by climbing L-shaped steps built of heavy boards to an L-shaped front porch, both wings of which were quite deep and wide. The door on the right was of solid dark-stained wood; it opened into the parlor room. The screen door on the left entered a wide hallway that divided the house. On the left were two bedrooms. On the right were two more bedrooms leading to a dining room, kitchen, and large pantry. The hallway itself led out to a back porch, at the far end of which was a well made of circular tile about three feet in diameter. Straight ahead from the well through a high gate was a smokehouse and a barn.

This was the setting, the arena in which I spent my youth, the formative years that psychologists dote upon. The milieu was town and country mingled. We lived on the edge of a village that I walked through almost every day. Each resident in the community was magnified because there was a limited number of them. Each person, each name, was important. And for three or four miles around, the fields and creeks and fragrant pine forest, as well as the inhabiting animals, domestic and wild, were free for my seeing.

It was here that I became a consumer in the world of print. Words on paper fascinated me more than spoken words. One person in particular was responsible for this, I believe—my maternal grandmother, Ann Elizabeth Cranford. She came to live with us soon after we moved into the house and my mother went to work in a local dry goods store. Although Grandmother Cranford was nearing eighty (and would live to be 101), she seemed never more than half her age physically, and her inquiring mind was interested in everything under the sun.

She had a fund of stories about her experiences—childhood in Tennessee (her father hunted with Davy Crockett), the covered-wagon trek to southwest Arkansas in 1849 (this was the year of the

Elizabeth Cranford, Dee Brown, Lula Cranford Brown, and Corinne Brown, about 1920

gold rush, but they liked Arkansas well enough that they decided not to go on to California), the Civil War in which she lost two brothers (at Shiloh and Stones River), General Steele's Yankee invaders in Ouachita County (Wild Bill Hickok was said to be one of their scouts who was captured in Camden), her cavalryman husband's capture in Tennessee and imprisonment at Rock Island, Illinois (he returned home mysteriously wearing parts of a Union Army uniform). Her husband, Henry Griffin Cranford, died when I was two years old, and my only memory of him is of a painted portrait that hung on the wall above my grandmother's bed.

She read widely—newspapers, magazines, an occasional book, her Bible especially. A frontier schoolteacher much of her adult life, she still kept a small collection of McGuffey's readers and Blue Back spellers on the top shelf of a cabinet in her bedroom. One afternoon soon after she came to live with us, she sat me down in her lap and opened a first-grade primer to a drawing of a running dog. Beneath the illustration were some little black marks that I had previously observed below or above pictures in books and magazines. My grandmother pointed to the little black marks in the primer. "The dog ran," she said slowly, tapping each of the printed three-letter words with a finger. And the mystic marks gradually became printed words: *The dog ran.*

I must have thought: "What magic is this? What wonder is this?" To me, the event was the discovery of a hidden secret that for some reason had been kept from me by conspiring adults. It was the most startling event of my childhood. Had that incident not been momentous I would not have remembered it all the rest of my days—the setting, in a room beside a window with a blooming apple tree outside, the picture of the running dog before me in the book, the mystery of reading suddenly unlocked.

From that moment I was an addict of the printed word, and addicts of the printed word, I eventually discovered, are almost certain to become compulsive writers hooked on pencils and pens and typewriters and nowadays marvelous contrivances called word processors.

My mother also was a reading addict, and she saw to it that plenty of good books were put in my way. By the time I started into the first grade I was devouring Robert Louis Stevenson and Mark Twain and had access to some of the great British authors of the nineteenth century—Dickens, Thackeray, Conrad—although I do not recall reading the latter until I was in school. Two of my aunts who lived nearby were subscribers to numerous magazines, and in that period when radio was in its infancy, movies were silent, and television had not yet been invented, the national periodicals were quite superior to the species seen nowadays on newsstands. Several of the better book publishers issued quality monthlies in which their forthcoming books often appeared in installments.

My paternal grandparents, Alexander and Mary Angelina Brown, lived on the other side of the town in a large U-shaped house surrounded by groves of oak trees and numerous beds of flowers. Beehives, which we were warned to stay clear of, stood in rows in an orchard some distance from the rear of the house. Alexander Brown was past eighty when we came there, and I recall almost nothing of his presence. He had been a lieutenant in a Louisiana light artillery regiment during the Civil War, had suffered a severe injury to a knee, and was captured at Port Hudson and paroled home to the war's end. After the war he refused to sign an oath of allegiance, quarreled with a carpetbagger government official, pulled the man's goatee, and had to flee to Texas until the carpetbagger departed.

My clearest memory of Grandmother Brown involves a trip to Mount Holly, some twenty miles to the southwest of Stephens, over an unpaved and unbridged road. The year must have been about 1915 or 1916. I don't recall the purpose of the journey; most likely it was to visit relatives on the Brown side. I know that it was proposed by Grandmother Brown because I remember that my mother was quite dismayed when she learned that we were going to travel in a two-seater horse-drawn hackney carriage. She protested that it would be better to hire the Gosden brothers' automobile— known as the town's jitney—and travel the twenty miles to Mount Holly in less than two hours and return home on the same day. But Grandmother Brown overruled all objections. She did not trust automobiles; they were always breaking down in the middle of nowhere. She probably wanted to spend the night there anyway. She persuaded her nephew (my cousin) Sam Thompson to drive the two-horse team, and off we went one morning on the sand and clay road to Mount Holly. Grandmother and Sam rode in the front seat, while my mother, my sister, and I were in the rear.

We had to spend the night in Mount Holly, of course, and must have started home late the next afternoon. Just at nightfall a terrific thunderstorm descended upon us without warning, the lightning and thunder frightening the horses. Cousin Sam Thompson and the two women frantically began putting up the canvas side curtains. The only light we had came from a kerosene lantern and frequent lightning flashes. With his calm voice, Sam tried to soothe the team, and he managed to keep them moving slowly forward until we came to one of the unbridged streams we had to cross.

There the team halted and stubbornly refused to enter a raging creek. Cousin Sam slapped the lines lightly against their rumps to urge them into the water. He probably feared they would bolt if he struck them too hard. Eventually he told Grandmother Brown that if she would hold the lines he would get out of the carriage and lead the horses across the creek. For a minute or so they disputed back and forth about the lantern. She wanted him to use it so that he could see where he was going, but—probably to reassure his passengers— he left it glowing feebly on the front floor of the carriage.

From the rear seat I watched him step out into blackness; then a quiver of lightning revealed his presence in front of the horses, pulling hard on the bridles to draw the team into the turbulent creek. My mother was clutching my sister and me, with one arm around each of us as though determined to save us if we were cast into the flood. Her fear was partly transmitted to me, I suppose, but at the same time I felt a sense of elation that I recall to this day. In order to see everything that was happening, I pulled away from her to peer over the back of the front seat. The lantern on the floor illuminated Grandmother Brown's feet, and in a dimmer light I could see her hands gripping the leather lines. Suddenly the carriage dipped forward and water rushed in, overturning the lantern and extinguishing it. In the blackness I heard Grandmother Brown gasp a suppressed "Oh!" My mother whispered something urgently behind me, and then, slowly, very slowly the carriage lifted out of the creek bed and we rolled onto level ground.

In a brief flash of lightning, Cousin Sam reappeared to take his place on the driver's seat. From shoulders to feet, his clothing dripped muddy water. Grandmother Brown turned to remark to my mother that if we had traveled by automobile we should all have been drowned. My mother did not say so, but I knew that she was thinking that if we had traveled by automobile we might have been safe and dry at home hours before.

I realized then that there was no more danger, and I think I regretted that it was past. Like the majority of human beings, I am a physical coward; this is nature's means of insuring perpetuation of the species. Yet for the first time I had discovered that there is something exhilarating about being in peril. Brashness sometimes saves lives, and too much caution can be fatal, but I do not recall during my youth ever deliberately going in pursuit of life-threatening hazards. Instead I sought dangers vicariously in print. The first hardcover book that I read—not long after the incident of the carriage in the flooded creek—was *Treasure Island.* I relished every perilous adventure that Jim Hawkins underwent in the search for buried treasure and surely enjoyed the tale the more because I, the young reader, had experienced danger myself and knew the surge of excitement that came from it.

Up the street from where we lived, just on the edge of the town's business section, was a printing plant from which came the weekly newspaper, the *Stephens News.* Once or twice a day I passed this building's wide-open door. Usually from this entrance came the sound of a clanking job press or the rackety rumble of a hand-powered flatbed press. But most alluring of all was the singular perfume of printing ink that floated out to permeate the air for several yards along the sidewalk. Compared to "all the perfumes of Arabia," nothing has ever matched the fragrance of printing ink in my nostrils. Unfortunately those delightful old inks vanished long ago, replaced by electronically controlled black powder and disagreeable chemicals that now press words upon paper.

After I grew old enough and daring enough to venture into that mysterious building of scented inks and drumming presses, instead of being chased out by a busy printer I was lifted upon a high stool, handed a composing stick, and shown how reversed metal letters were set and spaced to make words. When the gruff but kindly printer led me, still holding the composing stick, to a galley-proof press, rolled some of the aromatic ink over the type, and printed my name in black boldface, I knew that I had discovered another hidden marvel of the world that was almost as wonderful as the secret of reading. To this day print is not real print for me unless it is produced by metal letters inked with real printing ink impressed into the paper.

The overlord of the manufactory of print, I soon learned, was Mr. Charles J. Parker. Only his closest peers called him Charley to his face. He wrote most of the news and editorial matter and set some of the type. His sons—Charles, Jr. and Carleton—set most of the type by hand and operated the presses. I was in such awe of Mr. Charles J. Parker that I never spoke to him unless he spoke to me first. After all, in my small world he was the potentate of print and I a mere reader.

My first composition to appear in public print was published in Mr. Parker's *Stephens News*, probably in December 1918. One of the customs of the newspaper was to print letters shortly before Christmas from children to Santa Claus. The contents of these letters consisted mainly of a listing of Christmas presents desired, with an account of one's good deeds, promises to continue to be a good boy or girl, and perhaps a flattering line to Santa. I don't remember composing my letter, but I do recall the tingle of excitement when I first saw it in the newspaper's columns.

Each Friday afternoon that I was free to do so, I slipped into the printing plant to watch the birth of that week's *Stephens News*. Usually I sat on a metal box near the entrance, watching the Parker boys tightening and hammering the type forms, inking the press rollers, and then cranking out the first page proofs. One perfect set would be taken to their father's desk back in the rear. Other sheets less well inked or impressed too heavily or too lightly were thrown on the floor, from which I would retrieve copies. I felt it my duty to read every line in the newspaper, even miscellaneous matter printed from metal plates shipped from Chicago. Boilerplates they were

Annie Criner, Tom Criner, Matt Criner, and Lula Brown, in Stephens

called, and they usually contained a serial story, chapters from an adventure novel by Rex Beach, James Oliver Curwood, Zane Grey, B.M. Bower, or Mary Roberts Rinehart. These plates had to be fastened to column-wide supports that made them exactly type high. They could be inserted into any page of the paper, easing the weekly task of filling sixty-four or more columns of print with hand-set type.

Later on, after the coming of the oil boom that brought even more exciting activities, I became so busy that I seldom found time to visit the printing plant. One Friday, however, I dropped in for a visit and discovered that the Parkers were buying their paper stock for the *News* pre-printed on one side of the sheets and were no longer using mat plates. Somehow I viewed this as a betrayal of print, yet it did not diminish the high potentate of the newspaper in any way.

In addition to his renown as editor, Mr. Charles J. Parker was also a leading orator, chosen more often than any other to deliver speeches at Fourth of July celebrations, high school graduations, veterans' reunions, and so forth. In his office he worked in his shirt sleeves, but no matter how sultry the weather might be, he never appeared in public without his jacket and necktie. He was said to have told a visitor that the flapping of his light alpaca coat's sides and tails, when he gestured with his arms while orating, created a flow of air that kept him cool.

At that young age, I'm sure that I did not know the meaning—or even the spelling—of the word *surrogate,* but that is what I must have wanted Charles J. Parker to be—a surrogate father. He was too remote a figure, however, moving on too high a plane for me, and I'm certain that a few months after we moved away from Stephens he would not have recognized me or known my name.

Two uncles, married to sisters of my mother, became father substitutes, although I do not recall seeking out either of them for advice. They simply gave it unasked from time to time, and I may or may not have been an obedient nephew.

Uncle Tom and Aunt Annie Criner and their three sons lived about a hundred yards up the slope of hill from our house. Adjoining their town lots to the north was additional property, a sweep of countryside that began with a narrow open draw, or valley, where a stream ran from west to east out of a thick woods. Beyond the valley the ground rose to a thirty-acre orchard of peach trees that blossomed profusely in the springtime and produced an abundance of fruit in the autumns.

Uncle Tom could be crusty but was seldom ill-mannered. To insure respect from the young, he would bluster and ridicule, and during the first months I came to know him, I found him not only disagreeable but at times fearsome. After observing the attitudes and responses of his three sons, however, I learned that his actions were only pretensions and that underneath all that outward show of querulousness was a softhearted and generous human being. Reinforcing this feeling was the way Aunt Annie reacted during his stormiest outbursts. She remained as calm as the captain of a ship during a gale, paying a minimum of attention, moving steadily about her household duties, or reading quietly from a magazine or book until the eruption ceased.

As for the three sons—George, David, and Joe—whose ages ranged slightly above and below mine, they also generally adopted a policy of listening politely to their father's scoldings. Joe, the youngest and liveliest and most likely to get into trouble, sometimes would raise a question or two, but I never heard him offer excuses for any of the peccadilloes that made him a target for his father's wrath.

To generate income for his family, Uncle Tom operated a grocery store, although he spent much time dealing with other interests in timber, land, and a series of experimental endeavors that appealed to us all. For instance, when grapefruit were first marketed widely enough to be shipped to our little town, he admired the fruit's delectability and stocked them in his grocery store. Upon learning that a single tree could produce more than half a ton of fruit, he traveled to the Rio Grande Valley to investigate the prospects. On his return he talked of buying a grapefruit ranch. He made inquiries as to the practicality of growing grapefruit next to his peach orchard but soon abandoned that plan because the climate was not right.

Then he became fascinated by a little-known plant, the chufa nut, sometimes called ground almond. He read about it in one of the farm magazines, probably *Country Gentleman,* that recommended chufas as being the most inexpensive hog feed on earth. One spring he had all the open ground between his rows of peach trees plowed deep and planted in chufas, and while the crop was growing he purchased a considerable number of Poland China pigs.

Unfortunately some kind of porcine epidemic raging through the county destroyed most of the pigs before the chufa nuts ripened. I'm not certain what happened to that abundant crop, but I recall that my cousins and I pulled up numerous bunches, washed sand off the chufas in the creek, and chewed them vigorously. They tasted vaguely like almonds or chinquapins, but the hulls and nutmeats were so coarse that we spat out the residue rather than swallow it. Since that time, I have neither seen nor heard of a chufa nut.

When Uncle Tom decided to acquire an automobile, he went for the most exotic make he could find—a Cole Eight. This machine suddenly appeared one day in the grassy lane between our barn and the Criner barn. The Cole Eight was the longest car I had ever seen—shining, majestic, powerful. The leather upholstery exuded an odor of spices. Attached to the back of the front seats was a pair of drop seats, thus affording space for eight passengers. On each side of the rear interior were tall fluted flower vases, and when Aunt Annie was a passenger she always insisted that blossoms of some sort be placed in the vases.

Occasionally Uncle Tom organized trips to Camden, the county seat, twenty miles to the northeast over unpaved roads. Corinne and I always regarded an invitation to travel by automobile to Camden a rare privilege, although we had to arise at four A.M. and start out at first daylight. The running boards of the Cole Eight were always packed with tools, extra tires and tubes, tire-patching equipment, a shovel, several two-by-four boards, a supply of tow sacks, and an army blanket to place upon the ground when it became necessary to repair a flat tire or some mechanical failure beneath the car.

We always dressed in our best Sunday clothes for a trip to the county seat and tried to keep as neat as possible. We averaged one or two flat tires each way, and something would go wrong with the

Camden, Arkansas, around the turn of the century (courtesy Arkansas History Commission)

engine at least once. The only pavement in Ouachita County was on a few blocks of Camden streets, and when we arrived there, either Uncle Tom or George (who was then barely old enough to drive) would take us around on the smooth surface several minutes for the sheer pleasure of it.

Between Stephens and Camden there were a few stretches of deep sand, and two or three steep hills of red clay. The road through the sand was so deep-rutted that a driver could take his hands from the steering wheel and the car would steer itself. Sometimes we got stuck in a sanddrift, but a few tow sacks and two-by-fours and strong muscles would get us out. If two cars chanced to meet in these places, the drivers would have to climb out with their shovels and dig a diversionary route through the sand for one of the cars to pass. The red-clay hills were dreaded because they became slippery and impassable after rains, and if a hard rainstorm caught us on the return from Camden we sometimes stopped at the nearest house to spend the night. Wherever we might stop, the inhabitants usually would be related to someone in the car. It seemed to me that everybody in that part of Ouachita County was kin to everybody else, possibly because just three generations earlier many families from western Tennessee had immigrated there at the same time.

The brightest gem of all Uncle Tom's experiments was the building of his earthen dam that created the Great Pond. Around the time of the beginnings of the oil boom in 1920, he decided that the community needed a fishing pond. Employing a group of men who kept the county's dirt roads in repair, he set them to work with slips, scraping the earth for a dam from both sides of the little creek that ran through the narrow valley between the Criner house and the peach orchard. They soon had a dam in place, with a three-foot diameter tile in the center to serve as an outflow and a sluice gate for use when necessary. On the north side of the pond was a spillway that carried the normal stream flow around the dam.

One of the family legends that expanded in its tellings through the years concerned a near-fatal accident to Joe during the early days of testing the dam. When the pond first filled with water, it appeared that the spillway needed lowering to relieve pressure on the dam. A heavy rain made quick action necessary. To accomplish this, Uncle

Tom decided to open the sluice gate and drain the pond completely. When the heavy board gate was lifted at the opening of the three-foot metal culvert, the rush of water brought down a mass of brush and broken logs that began blocking the outflow pipe. Summoning everyone to follow, Uncle Tom led the way into the pond to begin clearing debris away from the opening. As usual, Joe jumped right into the midst of the action, and the whirl of water suddenly sucked him into the culvert. Knowing that the sluice was probably full of broken logs and branches that could stop the nine-year-old boy and drown him, everyone rushed to the top of the dam to watch the boil of water from the culvert's exit. Time stood still; then Joe bobbed to the surface riding on a log, looking very much like a red-haired Huckleberry Finn after the steamboat knocked him and Jim off their raft into the Mississippi.

As soon as the pond was at last properly filled, Uncle Tom stocked it with black bass and acquired a couple of rowboats. Fishing on the pond, especially in the flooded woods at the upper end where the water was shallow, was great fun and very productive. With the coming of the oil boom, however, fishing was relegated to a second place in the use of the pond.

Just as the summer of 1920 was beginning, hundreds of new people poured into the town, creating an urgent demand for a place to swim. The pond became a magnet, and Uncle Tom saw an opportunity to earn a few dollars. He quickly supplied the necessary equipment along with a few amenities. He built a pine-board structure that contained several dressing rooms, an office, and a veranda overlooking the water. In the deepest part, out near the dam, he erected a platform with a high diving tower. He ordered several dozen bathing suits of the now quaint 1920s styles to be sold or rented to customers. A large sign appeared on the side of the building facing the road: NATATORIUM. (I suspect that Aunt Annie found that classic name for him.) When he discovered that the oil workers wanted to swim at night, he strung electric lights around the structures.

With the passing of the oil boom, this grand creation gradually declined to shabbiness. Whether its demise had anything to do with Uncle Tom's decision to leave Stephens, I do not know. But soon afterward, he sold everything and took his family to Little Rock.

My other surrogate father, Charles Tutt, was almost an exact opposite in temperament to Tom Criner. Uncle Charley, a farmer and part-time logger, was married to my mother's youngest sister, who had been christened with an odd name, Brief. Aunt Brief was the most cheerful of the three sisters, very talkative and indulgent with children, perhaps because when I first knew her she had none of her own.

The Tutts lived about halfway between Stephens and Camden in a farmhouse set far back from the road. It was built in the style of the times for rural homes, with a wide-open hallway straight through the middle of the building. They were known as dogtrot, or shotgun, houses because the hallways were so wide that a shotgun could be fired from either end without a single pellet grazing a wall. (There are other definitions; the fancy modern term is breezeway.)

Because of the dense shade created by towering beeches, hickories, and oaks in the front yard, grass grew so sparsely that Aunt Brief had decided to keep the ground totally free of grass, leaves, and other litter. She had made several large brooms from brush, and one of the duties of young visitors was to sweep the yard clean every morning. Other country tasks assigned us included churning to make butter, picking wild blackberries, hoeing the vegetable garden, and feeding chickens and hogs. Some of these were the same as our home chores, but they seemed less burdensome at the Tutt farm.

In addition to the novelty of spending several days in the country, one of the joys of visiting the Tutts was traveling there by passenger train. In those days, for the convenience of passengers, conductors would stop local trains almost anywhere. When we boarded at Stephens we informed the conductor that our destination was not a town, but Finn Switch, a water tank only a mile or so from the Tutt farm. He would quickly figure the mileage, tell us our fare, and we would hand him a few coins, perhaps twenty cents. As we approached Finn Switch, he would pull the cord that ran through the cars to the locomotive engineer and the train would begin slowing with a great hissing of steam. Either Uncle Charley or Aunt Brief would be waiting there to walk us through the woods to the

Dee and Corinne in Hot Springs National Park, 1920

farmhouse.

For me the chief delight of riding a train was the opportunity it provided to obtain fresh reading materials. As soon as my companion or companions and I were seated, I went in search of the butch boy, or newsboy—that is, if he did not first come striding through the car, extolling his peanuts, candy, soda pop, and magazines. He usually kept his main supply of goods between two seats at one end of the smoking car, opposite the conductor's seat, a little nest of desirables, especially the dime novels. The dime novels' paper covers were garish scenes of frontier mayhem—Buffalo Bill, Jesse and Frank James, and Deadwood Dick. If I had two dimes to spare I would always buy two, and get my fill of frontier mythology, of which I believed every word in those pre-teenage years.

After Uncle Charley acquired a Model-T Ford, he and Aunt Brief would usually transport us by car to and from the farm, and the Finn Switch adventure virtually ended. One advantage of their owning the Ford, however, was that it increased our opportunities to visit Hot Springs. Uncle Charley evidently had more free time than Uncle Tom, and we visited the springs several times in his Model-T Ford. Along the way he would point out notable places, such as sites of minor Civil War actions, and a few miles outside Hot Springs he always stopped to show us the exact spot where many years before Jesse James had robbed a stagecoach. This, of course, added excitement to the journeys.

Before traveling to Hot Springs by automobile, we rode there on railroad trains. These were all-day ordeals for the adults, but I looked upon the transfers from one line to another over a distance of little more than a hundred miles as a series of grand adventures. (The three different railroads also offered a wider variety of dime novels for sale.) My mother and my aunts went to the springs mainly to take the mineral baths, which they believed would keep everybody healthy. We could not have afforded these visits except that a relative lived there and found places for everybody to bunk in her rambling old house.

I was entranced by Hot Springs and its tourist attractions—the alligator and ostrich farms, Happy Hollow amusement park, the wonderful trolleys and movie theaters—but I hated the baths and having to drink three cups of the sulfuric water every morning before breakfast. Hot Springs is where I purchased my first bound volume, for perhaps twenty-five cents in an antiquarian bookshop. The title is long forgotten, but it was one of those wild concoctions about the American Indian wars, a few facts mixed with numerous gory tales. I think it was the profusion of gaudy illustrations that attracted my attention—attacks on forts, arrow-studded corpses, old scouts being bound at the stake or staked out over anthills, wagon trains surrounded by fierce-faced Indian warriors.

Before we returned home, I read it through, and could not wait to show it to my peers. Young folk read a great deal more in that time than now, but what they got from it was probably no more uplifting or true to reality than the movies and TV shows they absorb today. An awful lot of bad writing was published in those days when print was king.

The few books that we youngsters owned were passed around until they were literally worn out, and by summer's end my book of Indian war horrors was a bit shaken, but so were all the Zane Greys and *Tarzan*s in our boys' own circulating library.

The public school I attended had no particular rules about the books we could bring to read during study periods. The teachers preferred us to borrow books from the tiny school library, but instead the boys brought their favorites and the girls brought theirs, passing them around as we did in the summer.

In the winter of the year that I turned twelve and was in the sixth grade, I witnessed my first book burning and was so horrified by the act that it has remained permanently fixed in my memory. One of the boys in my class asked me to bring the horrors-of-Indian-warfare book to school. I complied willingly, but I asked him to be careful and not to read it while Mr. Brennan was in the classroom. Mr. Brennan sometimes confiscated unassigned books and locked them in the teacher's desk, making it difficult to retrieve them.

Patrick Brennan was the school principal, a native of Ireland with a strong brogue, a burly man with a round flushed face. He taught all the mathematics classes, and every morning he came to instruct us in beginning algebra, remaining through a study period. His method of instruction was to inspire fear. He would send us to the blackboard, present a problem in his deep doomsday voice, and then would watch us squirm while we tried to solve it. Because of the anxiety he inspired in me, I rarely ever solved a blackboard problem. When the allotted time ended, he would come tramping down the aisle, pointing out the stupid errors we had made. Then he would ask that we present one of our hands palm up so that he might strike it a stinging blow with a twelve-inch ruler.

After algebra class on the day I brought the horrors-of-Indian-warfare book to school, I was studying for a geography test when I suddenly became aware of Patrick Brennan stalking slowly along the aisle across from me. He was approaching the desk of my friend, who, against my warning, was surreptitiously reading the Indian book behind his geography book, so engrossed in it that he was quite unaware that Brennan was behind and not in front of him.

A moment later, the book was in Brennan's hands. After a glance at the contents, he turned and strode over to the big wood-burning stove, which was in full blast against the winter cold. Without hesitation, he lifted the top of the stove and dropped the book into the inferno. To insure rapid conflagration, he opened the stove's damper.

I was stunned, enraged, murderous. If ever a book needed to be burned, perhaps that book was in a top category. But I could not believe it at the time.

Exactly when it was that I determined I must have my own printing press I am not certain. The idea arose from an advertisement that ran each month in one of the boys' magazines I received. Every time I read through a new issue, there it was—a picture of a hand printing press for sale by the Kelsey Press Company. After I wrote to learn the price, and found that the cheapest model, one with a three-by-five-inch chase, was twenty-five dollars (equal to twelve times that now), I realized that obtaining one was a faraway dream.

Then one spring day, quite unexpectedly, a magical solution materialized. Someone in the family suggested that the unused acreage beyond our vegetable garden should be the site of a work project for my cousin George and me. We would plow the ground, fertilize it, plant cottonseeds, hoe the rows regularly, pick the cotton, and haul it to the gin. The proceeds of the crop sale would be ours to keep.

At this distance in years, I can't imagine how we accomplished this. We surely had some help from time to time. In October, however, we delivered the crop to the local gin and received about twenty-five dollars apiece for our labors.

Of course I wanted to send my twenty-five off to the Kelsey Press Company, but I had already promised to use half of it to buy clothing for the coming school year. As my cousin George was the only one of my peers who had any spare cash, I approached him with a partnership plan. I convinced him that we could make all the money back, and much more, by printing stationery, business cards, and Christmas cards for friends, relatives, and acquaintances. (The advertisements for the press carried this assurance to back me up.) George saw the possibilities, and off went an order for a press with an accompanying can of printing ink and a font of type suitable for printing stationery and Christmas cards.

The days crawled by like unhurried terrapins; it seemed the press would never come. Then one day it finally arrived, packed carefully in a wooden box. When we got it unpacked, it seemed utterly insignificant when compared to the magnificent presses of Mr. Charles J. Parker. With it we found a small composing stick and a strip of metal type with instructions to place the letters and numerals in a cheaply made alphabetical case. To our dismay we could barely distinguish one letter from another. As we learned later, this was a font of Old English type, all capitals, the intricate face used by German printers until recent years. With great difficulty I set a line of type that I believed to be *Merry Christmas,* but after we locked it in the chase, inked the rubber rollers, and impressed the line upon a piece of paper, neither of us could be certain of what we had printed.

Next morning, we took everything over to the *Stephens News* building and presented our problem to Mr. Charles J. Parker. Although we thought of ourselves as potential competitors of his, we were relieved when he took pity upon us and advised us to return the Old English capitals to the press company and ask for a font of roman type, with both capital and lower-case letters. We followed his advice that very day.

While we were waiting for the new type to arrive, we became members of a newly organized Boy Scout troop, which for a time took our minds off the printing business. When the type did arrive— and a beautiful clear face it was—we used it to print announcements of Scout meetings, which we proudly distributed to the members. This inspired us to start a weekly paper, with news about the Scouts and whatever else we might wish to put into it. Who conceived the little newspaper's name, I do not recall, but the *Live Wire* had only a brief existence, seven or eight issues. Each page had to be set and printed, the type distributed and reset for another page.

I think it was the growth of the oil boom that killed the *Live Wire,* along with the tranquil ways of life in that isolated small town. Too much happened too quickly; there were too many demands upon the time and attention of everyone, adults and teenagers alike. No one among us could find the time every week to hand-set and distribute the type and print a small newspaper of four to eight pages.

Perhaps that halcyon period of my youth is idyllic only in memory. Yet two educational and entertainment organizations added fascinating and tantalizing bits of the outside world to our lives. Called chatauquas and lyceums, they presented their programs in the high school auditorium. Many families subscribed to these providers of lectures, music, and magic. In addition, each year the Paul English Players arrived with their big tent that they erected on the acreage of open grass high above the railroad tracks, the site used by circuses, carnivals, and medicine shows. Year after year Paul English gave us wonderful corny plays like *Charley's Aunt* and *Brewster's Millions.* We could see silent movies only on visits to larger towns.

The first radio set in Stephens was put together by a school-mate, J.B. Adams, with the help of his father. J.B. would invite one friend at a time to come by the Adams house to listen to a station in Pittsburgh that was on the air with music three hours each night. "It's like going to a lyceum program free of charge," J.B. would say while adjusting the earphones for his guests.

Yet all these novelties from the outer world did little to diminish the power of print upon us. Almost everybody read, by daylight if they had the time, by lamplight at night. Power lines did not bring electricity until after the oil boom.

Almost every family had a stereoscope with sets of viewing cards on various subjects. Each card had a pair of photographs taken at slightly different angles so that when viewed through the two eyepieces of the stereoscope, the scenery, animals, and people appeared to have three dimensions. Our set of cards consisted of photographs of Egypt and the Holy Land. Rainy Sunday afternoons were favorite times for stereoscope viewing, and if I grew weary of looking at pyramids and camels I would go visit my cousins, the Hammonds, who were fortunate enough to own a set of Wild West stereographs.

On summer evenings we gathered on front porches to watch the fireflies, study the stars and moon in the black sky, and listen to the symphony music of bullfrogs, crickets, tree insects, and hylas. In those leisurely hours there was a goodly amount of conversation, much of it based upon what we had read. Gossip in small towns is repetitious and can be dispensed with quickly, so there was not much of that.

Almost everybody attended church regularly. My family members and relatives were Church of Christ, Baptist, and Methodist. For me, the best things about religion were the revival meetings and the "all-day singings and dinners on the ground." The hellfire-and-damnation sermons gave me nightmares, but on summer Sundays when we went up to the Whitefield Church near Buena Vista it was like a grand picnic. Sessions of hymn singing were interspersed with sermons from midmorning until near sundown, but at noontime every family spread a long tablecloth on pine straw beneath the towering old trees and covered it with every imaginable variety of pies, cakes, meats, and large pitchers of milk and lemonade.

Revivals were usually held in large tents erected on the same greensward where the circuses set up theirs. The Methodist and Baptist revivals attracted the largest crowds and were the liveliest of those I attended, perhaps because they used loud pianos to accompany the voices. The Church of Christ used no musical instruments and chose more doleful hymns than the other congregations. At Methodist revivals, the younger set was seated together on a wide slanted platform, and we opened the services each evening with a very enthusiastic and emphatic rendition of "Brighten the Corner Where You Are." The Methodist sermons also seemed less ominous than most, and I do not recall suffering any nightmares after listening to them.

Fires were a continual menace to residences in those days before fire wagons and public water systems. One of the earliest fires that I remember was the burning of the nearby home of my relatives the Criners, up the slope from our house. As was usual the fire broke out at night, and I was awakened by the voices of my mother and grandmother shouting "Fire! Fire!" to summon help from neighbors before rushing to aid the Criners. Men, women and children formed a bucket brigade between our well and the burning house, and similar lines ran from wells at other houses, but the fire was soon out of control. For several weeks, the Criners lived in the two big rooms across the wide hall from the part of our house we occupied.

Soon after my cousins moved back into a new house built on the same site, another fire across town destroyed the home of the Northum family, and the husband, wife, and a young son moved into our two spare rooms. During their stay I found Mr. Northum to be the most fascinating adult I had known up to that time. He spent most of his days either working on, or talking with visitors about, a perpetual motion machine that he was confident he was very near perfecting. Mr. Northum had already invented a mechanical device that kept a record of long-distance telephone calls, and he and his family lived on the small royalties that the Bell Telephone Company paid him for use of the contraption.

This income also gave Mr. Northum time to experiment with perpetual motion machines. During the period that he lived with us, he kept busy fabricating various turning devices. I recall his receiving a large shipment of yardsticks and several boxes of toy train wheels and tracks. He worked much of the time in the cool shade of our back porch, building objects from the yardsticks and toy train parts. He constructed a wheel-shaped machine about four feet in diameter upon which he attached lead weights to toy wheels that rolled back and forth over short tracks as the apparatus revolved. With a slight push he would start his invention to turning on its axle. He would stand there beside it for what seemed like an hour, in an attitude of certainty that the machine would never stop. Yet it always did stop.

When visitors from out of town came to see him, as the result of correspondence perhaps, he would usually sit with them on our front porch to discuss his perpetual motion machine and its potential as an investment. The only times I saw him angry were when someone would bring up the fact that the U.S. Patent Office refused to accept any applications for a perpetual motion machine on the grounds that the laws of physics made such an invention impossible.

Mr. Northum had a well-worn copy of the Patent Office's statement on the subject, and he had written notes on the margins refuting each official contention. He would read these aloud and point out to his visitors that the Patent Office had tried to stop him from inventing the long-distance recorder for telephones, an invention that was working quite efficiently, thank you, sir.

After the Northums found a house in which to live, they left our rooms across the hallway, and I was sorry to see them go. For a long time I missed Mr. Northum's cheery whistle as he worked away with his screwdriver, pliers, and tack hammer, creating crude models of perpetual motion machines that he believed would make him and the rest of the world free of toil forever.

Railroad trains played a large role in our daily lives because almost everything we used was brought by trains, and our two major products, lumber and cotton, were shipped out on them. Salesmen from the outer world (called drummers then) came and went on passenger trains, and when we traveled somewhere we rode on the trains. The railroad was the St. Louis Southwestern, also known as the Cotton Belt Route. Its four daily passenger trains and numerous freight trains ran straight through the middle of Stephens and created an atmosphere of bustle that otherwise would not have been there. A special nightly express sped by without stopping. If one could keep awake until nearly midnight, the express could be seen streaking through the town with whistle moaning, leaving a shower of sparks and a twinkle of red lights in its wake. Everyone said it was filled with money boxes and important people bound for Mexico City. If I had owned a fortune, I would have given it all to ride that train into the mystery-laden southwestern land.

Other special trains appeared occasionally on one of the sidetracks, awaiting passage of a regular scheduled train. Among them were circuses and excursions, and during one exciting year, when I was eight or nine, there were carloads of soldiers wearing peaked khaki hats. They were going to the Rio Grande to hunt Pancho Villa. During one of these stops the soldiers tossed packs of hardtack to us, some of which we kept for months as treasures. I would have given another fortune to go with the soldiers, although I had nothing against Pancho Villa. From what I had read in magazines of his adventures, I classed him with Robin Hood.

During the summer season, one of the benefits the passenger trains brought to the young was financial improvement. At every scheduled arrival we would be at the railroad station with baskets of Uncle Tom Criner's peaches. We spaced ourselves along the cinder platform, shouting up at the passengers: "Fresh Elberta peaches! Two for a nickel!" Windows would go up, and hands offering nickels would come down.

Yes, indeed, railroad trains on their steel tracks were our umbilical cords to the outside world. They were our entertainers, our benefactors, our bringers of food, clothing, and printed matter. In 1920, they brought us the Great Oil Boom, and nothing was the same ever after.

Street Scene, Stephens, Ark.

Main Street, Stephens, Arkansas, before the oil boom (courtesy Steven Hanley)

CHAPTER TWO

Oil Booms and Flimflammers

A FEW MONTHS BEFORE THE BEGINNING OF THE OIL BOOM, my mother was appointed postmistress for Stephens. This was a boon for me because she allowed me to deliver the one or two special-delivery letters that arrived in a week. The dime that I received for delivering each letter would buy more then than a dollar will today and was my pay for other duties such as sweeping the post office floors every afternoon after school. Another assignment was to meet the early-morning passenger train before school and rush the first-class mailbag up the hill from the station to the post office.

Until the oil discovery, the only major problems facing the little post office were the seasonal arrivals of hundreds of bulky mail-order catalogs from Sears Roebuck and Montgomery Ward. Every family received one of each, most of them going out on the four rural mail routes. The mail carriers hated the catalogs almost as fiercely as did the local merchants. Some of the carriers used automobiles in dry weather; all used horse-drawn buggies when the roads were very muddy, and one man sometimes resorted to horseback, with a pair of saddlebags for the mail. Whatever mode of transport was used, several days were required for delivery of all the catalogs.

Soon after delivery the recipients would begin ordering various items, stopping the carriers along the roads to buy money orders, and this always added hours to the daily runs. Then, a few days later, an abundance of parcel post packages would arrive, further burdening the carriers. In the 1930s George Milburn wrote a short novel, *Catalogue*, about this recurring phenomenon in a contemporary Oklahoma town, describing how the merchants offered a dollar for every catalog turned in for a public burning on Main Street. Soon afterward there was an increased demand at the post office for penny postcards upon which requests were made to the mail-order companies for replacement catalogs. In Stephens the merchants offered a certain amount of goods for catalogs turned over to them, but I do not recall a public burning. More likely the catalogs were ripped apart and used as toilet paper in the outdoor privies.

The first oil strike in southwest Arkansas is so significant that its location three miles northeast of Stephens has been listed on the National Register of Historic Places. The well was not a gusher, but it had a high rate of flow. According to legend, a young man named Theo Norman had a vision of flowing oil while he was on a mountaintop in Montana, and this vision brought him to Ouachita County, Arkansas. After finding the location he had seen in his dream, he sought out a Louisiana wildcatter, S.S. Hunter, who persuaded two Stephens businessmen to assemble fifteen thousand leased acres. The well was named for the businessmen—Lester and Haltom No. 1.

Soon after the oil strike, strangers began arriving in town, a few in the beginning, then by the dozens. First came the rig builders to erect new wooden derricks, then the drillers, roustabouts, and roughnecks—wearing Texas hats, red corduroy shirts, and leather boots. We learned that you could distinguish drillers from ordinary roughnecks by the fact that drillers usually wore diamond rings and stickpins and favored bright-colored silk shirts and neckties. Oil scouts could be identified by their fancy leather jackets, which they wore as a sort of uniform. On the heels of this crowd came the lease hounds, wildcatters, oil smellers or professional geologists, traders, and promoters—we had to learn an entirely new vocabulary—and most of this latter group wore blue serge or seersucker suits and white shirts with detachable collars. They spent a lot of time figuring on the backs of envelopes and other bits of paper and generally were surrounded by blue clouds of smoke from their overpowering cigars. The oil people quickly filled up Miss Pearl Boggs' hotel, the only lodging place in town, sleeping six to a room or lined up on cots along the roofed porches. They overflowed into the residences of the town—into spare rooms and parlors—and the standard fifty cents per night for a bed rose to sixty cents, seventy-five cents, then a whole dollar.

All the while, freight trains were filling the switch tracks to

Oil well near Stephens, early 1920s (courtesy Arkansas History Commission)

unload drilling rigs, lumber for derricks, long flatbed wagons, mules, and a few automobile trucks. These undependable trucks and the very dependable mule-drawn wagons hauled steel casing to the oil wells and clogged the streets and roads, which quickly fell apart from the heavy traffic. After rains, every road out of town was a mud-bog, and as soon as the sun dried them they turned to powdered dust that smothered any traveler unlucky enough to be caught behind another moving vehicle. Out in the pine woods around the town rose forests of derricks. Lights glimmered all night from the crown blocks, and the rackety-clank and steady thudding of drilling machinery never ceased.

Occasionally we walked or rode bicycles out toward Smackover Creek to watch the roustabouts struggle with casing and rigging on the derrick floors. We were fascinated by the earthen slush pits, flowing with muddy water away from the well. If the well was nearing completion, the driller would come out frequently to the slush pit and thrust his fingers in it to smell and taste the flow. This wasn't a gusher field, but sometimes the first strike would shoot up to the crown block with a roar and then subside. The crude oil was dark brown—brown gold, the oilmen called it—and its pungent aroma was not unpleasant. The smell of money, the oilmen said.

Perhaps more than any other of my young companions, I was in a position to share, though minutely, in the sudden wealth that showered upon the town. The one or two special-delivery letters that I had been carrying each week quickly increased to several letters each day. It was not easy to find some of the addressees, all strangers, who might be boarding in somebody's house or living in one of the jerry-built pine-and-canvas shacks springing up along the railroad. About half of the letters, however, went to the cigar smokers in Boggs' Hotel, and occasionally one of the recipients there would corrupt me with a nickel tip.

The hotel was like a beehive, the long front porch filled with drones, their feet propped on the railing, their voices continually murmuring. The small lobby was always packed with busy figurers, a line of them formed at the hotel's only telephone. My daily visits improved my vocabulary of picturesque profanity as well as the exotic language of the oil fields. I learned the meanings of "a hundred acres of close-in stuff," "casing off the water" and "going down for new sand," "high-grade pools," "spudding in," "jammed casings," "dusters," "fishing for lost bits," "well logs," "under-rimming," "capping it," "bailing out" and "swabbing," and a new meaning for Christmas tree, which was an assembly of metal fittings used as a control device at the casing head of an oil well.

The increase in special-delivery letters was making me incredibly rich, sometimes as much as sixty cents a day, and my mother was so busy with the inundation of mail pouring into the Stephens post office that she did not realize I had become the foremost consumer of licorice sticks, jawbreakers, and ice cream cones in town. The Post Office Department had authorized employment of an assistant postmaster, a Mr. Marlar, and one of his duties was to keep the special-delivery record sheets and hand me the letters to deliver each morning and evening. My enormous income, therefore, was known only to him and me, and he evidently did not give it much thought until several weeks later.

At the height of the boom, the Stephens oil field began to attract its share of fast promoters and flimflam artists. The most romantic of these people was a pair of oil-stock peddlers named Jimmy Cox and Doc Ladd. With their flair for the dramatic, Cox and Ladd disdained to come to Stephens by way of the Cotton Belt Railroad. They arrived by airplane, a World War I Curtiss Jenny, landing in a cow pasture southwest of town. We had seen only one airplane before this; its passage from Pine Bluff to Texarkana was announced in the *Stephens News* and the entire town turned out to gaze upward at the plane's silhouette high in the sky as it kept its course by following the track of the railroad. The noisy chattering of its motor was impressive, but its remoteness was disappointing; it faded away no larger than a hawk against the horizon.

So when we learned that an airplane was actually going to *land* at Stephens, the excitement was intense, especially among the young who had heard and read so much about the heroic aviators of World War I. In the early twenties that war was quite fresh in our memories. We knew all about von Richthofen the Red Baron, Georges-Marie Guynemer the French ace, the Lafayette Escadrille, and our own Eddie Rickenbacker. And the rumors around town were that the men coming in on the Curtiss Jenny were not only important oilmen, they were also heroes of the skies who had fought Kaiser Bill and the Huns to Make the World Safe for Democracy.

As I recall, Cox and Ladd's Curtiss Jenny arrived a bit earlier than expected, but we had been waiting for hours in the pasture for that wonderful event, and it happened so fast that the plane was down, rolling, and bumping across the uneven surface of the pasture almost before we heard or saw it. On the ground it resembled a fragile insect made of spruce, linen, and wire, leaping swiftly toward a ditch where its nose tipped forward, its tail pointing skyward like a snake doctor on a lily pad. As the crowd of boys swarmed toward the plane, a spray of broken wood from a splintered propeller miraculously missed all of us. Half a dozen boys, including me, managed to retrieve some of the pieces as we ran; my souvenir of the broken propeller was a splinter of polished mahogany the size of a hammer handle.

We could see the leather-helmeted skulls of the plane's two occupants. A slim young man crawled out first; he pushed his goggles back on his forehead. He wore a yellow silk scarf around his neck. His tight-waisted leather jacket reached below his knees, almost concealing his neatly pressed officer's trousers. Behind him was a stocky heavy-set man who was turning to lift a fat bulldog from the cockpit. The heavy-set man wore pants that flared at the hips and tightened at the knees; his lower legs were encased in leather military puttees. The slim man walked around to inspect the broken propeller. He uttered a few swear words and said they would have to send a telegram to San Antonio for a replacement. The stocky man was grumbling about a jammed elevator wire, which he hoped they could repair themselves.

By this time Mr. Charley Parker the editor, and Daddy Brummett the town marshal, and several other important citizens of Stephens had pushed up to welcome the arrivals and to clear youngsters out of the way. We pressed close enough, however, to learn that the slender man was Jimmy Cox, the stocky man Doc Ladd. Jimmy Cox walked with a limp, supporting the rumors we had already heard that he had been wounded in a dogfight with the German ace, the Red Baron.

Within a few days after their arrival, Cox and Ladd and their bulldog had ingratiated themselves into the hearts of the citizens of Stephens. They wasted no time hobnobbing with oil people like themselves. Instead they mingled with us, spending time meeting representatives of the town's business and professional interests, swapping stories with the local war veterans, and even attending church—at least once. They lingered about the street corners, the drugstores, the cafes. They opened an account at the bank. They came into the post office, introduced themselves, and rented one of the oversized mail boxes. All the businessmen in town and a few families rented post office boxes; others got their mail at the general delivery window, which I sometimes manned for an hour or so at noontime when my mother or her assistant went out for lunch. We had only two oversized boxes. The *Stephens News* rented one, but the other box had remained unrented until Cox and Ladd arrived. We all wondered why they would need such a large box. We soon found out.

A few days later Cox and Ladd were joined by a driller and a pair of roughnecks who had traveled from Texas in an Oilfield Special, a Dodge roadster with high axles designed for deep-rutted roads. They now set up headquarters in a brand-new two-story brick building which some of the town's enterprising businessmen had rushed to completion. The building was on Main Street, and Cox and Ladd rented an entire office suite. To occupy the desks, four or five young women arrived suddenly one day from Texas. I thought they were the prettiest girls I had ever seen. They wore jaunty tam-o'-shanters, low-cut shirtwaists, and skirts short enough to expose half the calves of their white-stockinged legs. The also used considerably more rouge than did the local girls. To me they were the same as movie stars, although I didn't know much about movie stars, having seen only a few movies in theaters at Camden and Hot Springs. But then everything connected with Cox and Ladd was glamourous. The debonair pair had already entered my pantheon of legendary heroes—right alongside Robin Hood, Jesse James, Buffalo Bill, Huckleberry Finn, and Eddie Rickenbacker.

About this same time, other developments were making life more interesting. A man named Ben Couch came over from Magnolia and leased the single remaining vacant lot on Main Street (which was between two solid-walled brick buildings). He boarded up the front and rear, built several rows of backless wooden seats, and set a white screen at one end and a projection booth at the other. There was no roof, but it was Stephens' first movie theater, its front always plastered with bright-colored posters of cowboys, Indians, bathing beauties, and scenes of violent action. The shows changed every night, and I was there every night that my mother would let me go. The admission price was no problem for me—a mere dime— as I was averaging at least six of them a day with my special-delivery letters.

Another outlet for my excess cash was a magazine stand. Instead of being in a drugstore as would be the case today, Stephens' first magazine stand was in Lawler and Pruitt's barber shop. Rather than furnish free magazines to beguile waiting customers, the barber shop offered them for sale. Before the installation of this wonderful array of gaudy-covered pulp magazines, my knowledge of periodicals was confined mainly to *Youth's Companion, American Boy, Saturday Evening Post, Country Gentleman, Literary Digest,* and several women's magazines that I seldom read. Most of these fine publications are dead now, victims of an age of nonreaders. Lawler and Pruitt's newsstand introduced me to a hundred more—*Wild West Weekly, Adventure Stories, Action Stories, Weird Stories, Black Mask,* and my favorite, the *Police Gazette.*

The *Police Gazette* was printed on pink paper and opened up a world I never knew existed—gruesome crimes, prizefighting, and sex. The covers varied from fierce-faced prizefighters to simpering bathing beauties, but the advertisements were the most fascinating part of the magazine. I was familiar with the Pen Pals section of *American Boy* where one could find addresses of boys who wanted to become pen pals. The Pen Pals column of *Police Gazette* was quite different. It listed *girls* who wanted to be pen pals with boys; object—matrimony. One of these advertisements was particularly appealing to me. For twenty-five cents one could obtain photographs and addresses of a hundred *señoritas* whose fathers owned ranches in Mexico, and it was boldly suggested that correspondents could become engaged to those *señoritas,* marry them, and eventually inherit cattle ranches. As one of my dreams was to become a cowboy, I sent for the pictures and addresses and wrote to two or three of the beautiful *señoritas*. But alas, no reply ever came. Of course, I knew no Spanish, and perhaps the *señoritas* could not read English.

One summer day I was stationed at the post office's general delivery window while my mother went home for lunch. Mr. Marlar, the assistant postmaster, was in the back, sorting circulars for the rural mail routes. Few people came for mail at midday, and I was deeply absorbed in a grisly love-triangle murder in the *Police Gazette* when an ethereal feminine face suddenly filled the window. She was one of Cox and Ladd's office girls, and she wanted to purchase ten thousand penny postcards. I called Mr. Marlar. He checked the supply, and informed her that we had less than a thousand in stock. The outcome of this was that Cox and Ladd had to travel in their Dodge Oilfield Special to several post offices up and down the Cotton Belt Railroad until they collected their ten thousand postcards. Not long after this, the Cox and Ladd girls brought in the ten thousand cards to be mailed. These postcards had been run through the *Stephens News* job press and contained an exciting printed message composed by Jimmy Cox. They were addressed to people all over the country, but the majority were going to California, a heavy concentration to Pasadena. Many of the addressees were doctors and dentists, and I understand that to this day doctors and dentists still have a weakness for hot oil stocks. For that is what Cox and Ladd were selling. Not long after the cards went out, several thousand copies of a special edition of the *Stephens News* containing a two-column announcement of Cox and Ladd's glorious oil enterprises were mailed—very probably to the same sucker list.

Needless to say, the avalanche of postcards and newspapers (which were rolled in penny wrappers) created a problem for the Stephens post office, which normally dispatched no more than a hundred pieces of mail each day. We had only one hand stamp canceler, and not only I but the three rural mail carriers had to be drafted to assist in the tiresome drudgery of canceling the drift-heap of outgoing mail from Cox and Ladd.

Jimmy Cox wrote all the oil-stock sales copy, and I believe his was the first writing style I ever attempted to imitate. In fact, I was not aware that there was such a thing as a writing style until I'd read the literary compositions of Jimmy Cox. He kept his relationships with his suckers on a highly personal level, greeting them as "pardners," confiding in them his discovery of what might be the largest "mother pool" of oil in the world, and giving them the first chance at a once-in-a-lifetime opportunity to make a fortune beyond their wildest dreams. He assured them that Cox and Ladd could dive deeper and come up with more oil profits than any wildcatters in the business. For a limited time only, the inside "pardners" could send a check for one share, two shares, a hundred shares, or more before this opportunity for sure riches would be opened to the general public. The complimentary close to his message struck me as being a piece of literary genius: "Fortune smiles but tempus fugits."

Not long after the first series of mailings went out, an unusual number of letters began arriving from California and elsewhere addressed to Cox and Ladd. And a surprising number of letters came special delivery. One morning about thirty arrived. The next day forty or fifty. To earn four or five dollars (and remember that was equal to what forty or fifty dollars will buy now), all I had to do was walk around the corner each morning, enter the new brick building on Main Street, and hand a packet of special-delivery letters to one of the spicily perfumed young ladies in the office of Cox and Ladd. Suddenly I had enough money to buy the expensive camera I'd been wanting, and I could visualize a new bicycle only a week or so away.

But it was too good to last. One afternoon my mother called me back to the rear of the post office and showed me the special-delivery record sheets. She explained to me that on some days I earned more money than Mr. Marlar, the assistant postmaster. She had been attempting to obtain an increase for him, she said, but the Post Office Department had turned down the request, suggesting that the rise in special deliveries resulting from the Stephens oil boom might well be added to his income. I protested that I needed the money, too, for a bicycle. We compromised. In the future I could deliver one letter per day. Mr. Marlar would deliver the remainder.

This was the sort of financial blow that drives men to desperation. My pockets no longer jingled with coins. I was practically a pauper. I cast about for a way to recoup, and at first I could think of nothing. But because I had this brand-new camera, I answered an ad in the *Police Gazette*. The ad read: BECOME A PROFESSIONAL PHOTOGRAPHER AND EARN BIG MONEY. I sent off for the instructions, enclosing one of my precious dimes. The manual came. I read it and went out with my camera to earn big money. I photographed a railroad bridge and an oil derrick, and then, because the manual said that animals make appealing subjects, I began concentrating on neighborhood cats and dogs. I found an old hound asleep by the Methodist Church, and while I was trying to get him to pose for me, a girl suddenly appeared, demanding to know what I was doing. She was one of a pair of twins, Sharon and Tharon, daughters of an oil driller, and a year or two ahead of me in school. I was much in awe of that pair of sophisticated red-headed Texas girls who must have been all of fourteen years old. They were identical twins, seldom apart, and to this day I don't know whether it was Sharon or Tharon who graciously lifted the head of the sleepy hound for me to photograph. Anyway, when I received the first prints I discovered that in my nervousness I had missed most of the hound, but had a sharp close-up of Sharon or Tharon. The snapshot of her pretty face was so splendid that I put it away in a secret place to be taken out and admired only on special occasions.

It was about this time that I received a flash of inspiration, one of those once-in-a-lifetime creative ideas that lead on to fortune. It occurred to me that if some people would send Jimmy Cox and Doc Ladd big checks for stock in an oil well that they weren't even sure existed, and that some other people would send off twenty-five cents to obtain a list of Mexican *señoritas* who never answered their mail, then it was about time for me to get into the business. I did not know then what the word flimflam meant, but I was about to join the flimflam artists of Arkansas's first oil boom.

Withdrawing the few dollars savings that I had been encouraged to deposit in the Bank of Stephens when I was in the big money, I sent off some advertising copy written in the dashing style of Jimmy Cox to both the *Police Gazette* and *American Boy*. It went something like this:

FIND YOURSELF A SWEETHEART BY MAIL. *Hundreds of Warm-Blooded American Beauties* Whose Fathers Are Making Millions in the Oil Fields. Send only *25 cents* for Sample Snapshot. Satisfaction Guaranteed. GOLDEN HORSESHOE AGENCY. GENERAL DELIVERY. STEPHENS, ARKANSAS.

American Boy returned the advertising copy with a curt statement that they did not publish advertising of that sort, but the *Police Gazette* let it pass. Since I was still stationed most noontimes at the general delivery window, it was no problem watching the *G* pigeonhole for mail addressed to my Golden Horseshoe Agency. I was startled when I found the first letter there and slid it with thumping heart into one of my pockets. I was even more startled when I opened the letter later and found a silver quarter and a request for a sample snapshot of an American beauty whose father was making millions in the Stephens oil boom.

Of course the only snapshot I had to send was that one print of beautiful Sharon, or Tharon, and I didn't want to give it up. But I rushed off the negative to a photo processing company, enclosing the last remaining reserves of my vanishing capital to pay for additional prints of the oil driller's twin daughter. By the time the prints arrived, I had received fifteen or twenty more letters with silver quarters in them. The total receipts came to about what I had invested in the advertisement, and I was also out the cost of photo prints and postage stamps. But I was not dismayed. That is, not until I received a letter of reply from one of my clients demanding to know the name and address of the girl whose snapshot I had sent him. He was from somewhere up in the hills of Kentucky, and he enclosed a photograph of himself for me to pass on to the girl. He was a rawboned, slightly balding man of about forty, his irregular teeth showing slightly in a forced smile. He wore no collar or tie, but his shirt was held together at the neck by a gold collar button.

This was an eventuality I had not foreseen, and I pondered over the problem for two or three days, wondering how Jimmy Cox would handle it. In my mind I composed two or three replies to the love-stricken Kentuckian, but none of them seemed suitable. Then one morning, when I reported to the post office to see if there might be a special-delivery letter for me to carry, I found my mother and Mr. Marlar in a state of high excitement. They had received a telegram from the inspection division of the Post Office Department stating that a fraud order had been issued against Cox and Ladd. Their post office box was to be sealed, and all their mail held pending arrival of a postal inspector. What all this meant did not sink in on me at first. In the beginning I thought what a pity it was that all those stacks of special-delivery letters had to be held there in the post office; they represented dimes that neither Mr. Marlar nor I could collect.

Not until after the arrival of the postal inspector, followed by a buzz of rumors that our beloved folk heroes, Jimmy Cox and Doc Ladd, and their bevy of beautiful office girls might all be thrown into prison for selling worthless oil stock, not until then did I realize that what I had been doing was flimflamming the public by mail just as they had been doing. The Golden Horseshoe Agency did not have a post office box, and I did not see how the G pigeonhole of the general delivery window could be sealed, but I feared that it was possible a fraud order might be issued against the Golden Horseshoe Agency. Although I was the only person in town who knew it, the Golden Horseshoe Agency was me. Not even the prospect of sharing a cell in Leavenworth prison with my heroes, Jimmy Cox and Doc Ladd, could relieve the anxiety that weighed upon me.

Fortunately I still had the fifteen or so silver quarters received by the Golden Horseshoe Agency, and I wasted no time sealing them up in plain envelopes and addressing them back to the eager gentlemen who had sent them to me in exchange for a snapshot of Sharon, or Tharon. I made no explanation other than that the Golden Horseshoe Agency had gone out of business. After surreptitiously putting all these letters into the drop at the post office, I breathed easier, and as the days passed and no more mail for the Golden Horseshoe Agency appeared in the G pigeonhole, I was sure that I had escaped the troubles besetting Cox and Ladd.

And then one day I found another letter from that amorous Kentuckian. He was sorry, he wrote, that the Golden Horseshoe Agency had gone out of business because he had fallen in love with the girl whose photograph we had sent him. He just had to know her name and address or go crazy because he thought about her all the time, and if it was the last thing he ever did he was going to marry her. He reckoned that if we did not send her name and address he would just have to get on a train and come to Stephens to find her himself.

That letter naturally put me into a state of dread. I could picture that rawboned Kentuckian stalking off a train and colliding head-on—not with the *single* object of his desire but with a pair of them—Sharon and Tharon together. What would happen after that was beyond the limits of my young imagination. Each day during my noontime duties at the general delivery window I expected to be confronted by that mountaineer's face looming up and demanding to know where he could find the Golden Horseshoe Agency. But if he ever came to Stephens I never knew of it, and the Golden Horseshoe Agency did not hear from him again.

So concerned was I with the bursting of my own flimflam bubble, I scarcely realized what was happening to Cox and Ladd. I was almost unaware, too, that the Stephens oil boom was dying—the roustabouts, drillers, scouts, and promoters flocking away to El Dorado, Norphlet, and Smackover. The number of special-delivery letters arriving in the mail soon dropped back to one a week, and then I knew that the boom was ended. Meanwhile, the offices of Cox and Ladd were closed, they too departing for new fields to wildcat while awaiting trial for their flimflam game.

Later on, like almost everyone else in Stephens, I was grieved to hear the news that Jimmy Cox and Doc Ladd had been sentenced to prison. Regardless of what wrongs they may have committed in their merry and swaggering appeals to mankind's natural greed, they had brought into our placid lives more glamour than had ever touched us before. For me, they will always be men of magic, true artists at flimflam games, the legendary giants of that brief but eventful oil boom of my youth.

CHAPTER THREE

Little Rock in the Roaring Twenties

IN THE SUMMER OF 1924, we moved to Little Rock, mainly because my mother wanted Corinne and me to obtain good high school educations. The high school that we attended was not the Central High of the notorious 1957 desegregation conflict but was called simply Little Rock High School.

I do not know whether or not the Little Rock schooling was any better than we had been receiving, but downtown there was a splendid public library that in those more literate times was warmly supported by a majority of the citizens and their elected officials. The library became almost a second home for me. I read far more from the library's collections than I did in school, perhaps because I did the choosing.

On one occasion, however, a school librarian pointed me to a three-volume set of books that started me upon a course that I was to follow into my career as a writer. For this, I have always been most grateful to her. The title of the set was *History of the Expedition Under the Command of Captains Lewis & Clark.* It was far more exciting than any dime novel, or even Stevenson's *Treasure Island,* which it somewhat resembled in style and structure and suspense. This was the *real* American West that I was encountering for the first time.

It has been said that the most enduring works of literature are stories of journeys in which the chief interest of the narrative centers around the adventures of the hero or heroine. If this be true, there is no greater adventure story in American history than the expedition of Meriwether Lewis and William Clark, a journey filled with danger, mystery, romance, and grueling suspense. Instead of one hero it contains several, and one sterling heroine, the Shoshone woman, Sacajawea, without whose aid they might not have reached their destination.

The school librarian, who was also a teacher in those days, loaned the three volumes to me one at a time. There began my first real interest in the history of my country, and in the American West in particular.

By chance during my high school years, I discovered two writers of my own time who were to influence my view of American life and literature. It came about in this way. To reach the school, which was on the east side of the city two miles from where we lived, we either rode a trolley car or walked. The fare was five cents, but if the weather was good, most of the boys in my neighborhood walked in order to save the nickel for candy bars or movie tickets. On those mornings I began to notice a plump little man hurrying in the opposite direction, toward the nearest trolley-car stop. One day he was reading a book as he approached, balancing it on his slight paunch and occasionally glancing briefly over the top of his glasses to make certain of his footing.

Next morning he was still reading the same book, and my curiosity was aroused as to what could be so absorbing that he was compelled to read while walking to the trolley stop. On the third morning I saw that he was near the last pages of the book. If I was to know its title, I must follow him. Deciding to sacrifice my five cents, I followed him aboard the streetcar. While he was paying his fare, I caught a glimpse of the book's title—*Winesburg, Ohio,* by Sherwood Anderson. Furthermore, the sticker on the volume's spine told me it was a library book.

Within the week, *Winesburg, Ohio* was in my hands, and I soon discovered why the rotund stranger could not wait to reach his seat on the trolley to continue his reading. I do not know if he was from a small town, as I was, but I suspect he was. Although Anderson's Ohio was foreign to me, most of the characters in his book were as familiar as if they had been flesh and blood. Yet being still a teenager, I knew only the surfaces of the parallel characters in my small town. Anderson told me the secrets of their lives—the meanness and goodness of small-town America. I identified with his main character, George Willard, who was really Anderson himself.

Over the years that followed, I read everything I could find that

Sherwood Anderson published. More than a decade later, while I was living in Washington, D.C. during the 1930s, I finally met him—in somebody's apartment, at one of those numerous little gatherings that were always being held for some cause or other in those yeasty days of President Franklin Roosevelt's New Deal.

Anderson was the guest of honor, of course, writers being highly esteemed by the Roosevelt administration (but shunned by all others since, except during the brief reign of John F. Kennedy). He said a few words to the group, something about Washington being the only place in America where everybody was important, therefore nobody there was important. He had recently acquired two weekly newspapers in Marion, Virginia—one Democratic, the other Republican—and when I found an opportunity to talk alone with him I said that my lifelong dream was to own a country weekly. That had been an early dream for him, also, he said, but he had been unable to achieve it until he received a little money for a novel that had sold better than most of his other books. Also, he had no magic formula for me to follow his example, but he invited me to visit his printing shop in Marion, and I later did so.

Shortly after I reluctantly returned the copy of *Winesburg, Ohio,* I discovered John Dos Passos in the public library. The first book I read was *Manhattan Transfer,* a realistic treatment of New York and its area. I was fascinated by the introductory passages to the chapters, a technique that he later brought to perfection in the "newsreel" and "camera eye" sections of his U.S.A. trilogy. I did not shift my allegiance from Anderson to Dos Passos, however, until the trilogy was completed, the first volume appearing while I was in college. These works struck me with the effect of lightning bolts because of their treatment of contemporary American life. I read and reread them until I knew parts of them by heart.

Later, of course, I discovered Faulkner, and then Joseph Conrad, who together with Anderson and Dos Passos and the translators of the King James version of the Bible influenced me most. Writers do not spring full-grown from the forehead of Zeus. They are the products of family members, friends, teachers, and other writers. These human forces were all a part of the process that moved my pen across the pages of manuscript after I found my own subject niche in the nineteenth-century American frontier.

Although I was fortunate to stumble upon some of the better contemporary writers while in high school, I was also still reading my favorite pulp magazines—especially during the long summers. In an issue of *Blue Book,* I noticed an announcement that the editor would pay a hundred dollars for two-thousand-word stories of real adventure. A hundred dollars then was equal to more than a thousand dollars now, and I immediately set about concocting a story of "real adventure."

We lived only two blocks from the Arkansas Travelers' ballpark, and baseball was then the most real adventure I knew about. Creating a story around an actual scene I had witnessed in front of the home team's dugout, I told it from the viewpoint of a shortstop who was supposed to be me. The plot involved a rookie pitcher, a conceited sportswriter, the sportswriter's girlfriend, and her dog. A few weeks after mailing it to *Blue Book,* I received a check for one hundred dollars. Being only seventeen, I was absolutely certain that I had it made for life.

Disillusionment was not long in coming, however. Rejection slips soon taught me that no writer ever has it made for life. In fact, I learned that writing and baseball have much in common. Every time one goes to bat, it's a new ball game. A home-run hitter will strike out or pop up more than he will slam one over the fence or into the stands, whether it be a baseball or a manuscript.

Yet during the next two years, I did sell two more stories of "real adventure" to *Blue Book,* slightly changing my name each time, although I doubt if that fooled the editor, Donald Kennicott, who seemed to be genuinely interested in beginning writers.

Baseball was the outdoor mania of the teenaged boys of my neighborhood. When the Travelers team was not in town for us to watch, we usually played on a vacant lot near the ballpark. There were no "little leagues" in those times, no adults to supervise us, but someone was usually available to umpire and keep our batting averages, a record we considered very important.

For summer jobs, most of us sought morning employment so that we would be free for baseball by midafternoon. Night baseball had not yet been inflicted upon the fans. During two summers I worked as an iceman's helper. Though electric refrigerators had been introduced, the early models were expensive and not very efficient, and only a few families had them. The housewives posted cards in their street windows, indicating the number of pounds of ice they wanted each day. A twenty-five-pound block was easy to carry, but I hated the fifty-pounders. Each day we started out at dawn and were usually finished by noon.

Getting into a seat in the ballpark required strategy and fast footwork. Few of the members of my gang ever had money to spare for tickets, and even if we had, we would have been very reluctant to spend it that way. The ballpark had a long-standing rule that any baseball knocked over the fence in batting practice or during a game could be presented at the gate as admission to the bleachers. Because of its short outfield and low board fence, quite a few balls went out of that park. Consequently, an hour before game time, a group of eager youths was always gathered outside the very short left-field fence.

Luck played a large part in the retrieval of over-the-fence fly balls, but skill at catching them increased one's chances on days when the competition was keen. Most of us brought along our gloves; yet even so, on many days luck deserted us and we had to retreat up the slope to climb a tree from which we could see only about half the ball field, a considerable distance away.

Our fortunes improved considerably the summer that Moses Yellowhorse joined the Travelers. Yellowhorse may have been Osage, maybe Pawnee, I don't recall, but he had a pure Indian face that must have intimidated opposing batters when he put on his scowl and fired one of his fastballs over the plate. He had played for one of the big-league teams but had a tendency to walk too many batters, which is probably the reason he was sent down to the Southern Association. Yellowhorse spent much of his time in the bull pen, warming up to relieve the other pitchers.

Instead of the eight-foot board wall that surrounded most of the ballpark, a close-meshed wire fence ran along part of the bull pen. Because of a bleachers-supporting wall, the playing field could not be seen from outside the wire fence; but if we had not been lucky enough to catch a ball and get inside, we could stand near the wire and watch the pitchers warm up. They had a small roofed shed to sit in, and sometimes they would talk to us.

From the very first day I saw him, Moses Yellowhorse fascinated me. During the oil boom at Stephens, several Indians had come from Oklahoma to work on the rigs, and a Creek boy had been one of my closest friends in school there. After his family returned to Oklahoma, I visited him in Muskogee one summer. He liked to say that his people belonged to one of the "five civilized tribes," and that he was not what he termed a "wild" Indian. Yellowhorse was a "wild" Indian by those standards, being Osage or Pawnee, with a chiseled nose and a face that turned ferocious when he wanted it to. If he was not warming up, he liked to watch us try for those fly balls over the fence, and he would gravely applaud when one of us caught or snagged a ball that would let us in to see the game.

One day, after the game had started and I was lingering in hopes that a high foul might come floating over the fence, I noticed Yellowhorse watching me. He was sitting alone in the shelter, idly flipping a ball up and down. He got up and walked close to the wire fence. "Hey, kid," he said quietly, and tossed the ball over the fence. I caught it easily and must have stared at him in astonishment at what he had done.

He winked but kept a solemn face. "Take the ball in, kid," he said. "See the game."

That was not the only time. It became a sort of daily ritual, between him and me and one or two other boys. What he did, did not harm the baseball team's owners. The Travelers lost no money or baseballs. Yellowhorse delighted in our joy, and we delighted in his Indian "giveaways." He went on to show us how to hold the ball for various pitches—sliders, fast drops, and so on.

As a teenager nearly seventy years ago, I learned from Moses Yellowhorse that American Indians, even fierce-looking ones, could be kind and generous and good-humored—and faithful friends. From that time, I scorned all the blood-and-thunder tales of frontier Indian savagery, and when I went to the Western movies on Saturday afternoons, I cheered the warriors who were always cast as villains.

My peers and I engaged in the usual harum-scarum activities of boys
of that era. Most of the members of our "gang," including my Criner
cousins, lived on Schiller between Twelfth and Sixteenth streets,
with a few boys scattered in the neighborhood along Park and
Summit. Our gang was no organized group, its various segments
preferring different activities. For example, not all of us played
baseball. Certain ones would not engage in the back-lot shinny
games with tin cans. Only a few went in for wrestling and touch
football. But for the Saturday morning ritual of freight-train hop-
ping—which was strictly forbidden to all of us—every teenaged boy
in the neighborhood who could slip away from home would appear
in the railroad switching yard below the baseball park. No word
went out, yet every one of us seemed to know that at midmorning
a train-hopping expedition would be going up the river.

Among my favorite gang members was David Steel. He was a
preacher's son, and he tried to play the role of "bad boy" to the hilt,
but never quite succeeded. (In his adult life he was a petroleum
chemist and geologist and was one of the discoverers of the great oil
fields of north Africa.) There were also a doctor's son, an engineer's
son, a barber's son, and two sons of a merchant. Today, several of
us would be classified as members of "blue collar" families, but in
that time and place the concept of the middle class had not yet
evolved. We lived in a classless world.

None of us were terrorists or miscreants; instead, even in their
youthful anarchism, several were very interesting as individuals.
One of the Elliot boys, for example, was always surprising us with
his mechanical abilities. His father owned a small automobile repair
shop right there in the residential area, on Fifteenth Street, and
nobody objected to its presence because cars of that era were always
in need of mechanics, and the closer at hand they were the better.

This Elliot boy, in his middle teens, invented a device that might
have made him wealthy had the technology of radio not been
moving so swiftly in the 1920s. When he began working on his
invention, almost every family owned a radio (Atwater Kent and
Crosley were the big names) and the objective was to tune in as many
distant broadcasting stations as possible. People would brag about
picking up Chicago or Cincinnati or Kansas City, but the problem

was that listeners did not know what city they had tuned in until an announcer spoke at the end of the program. To solve this difficulty, the Elliot boy removed the front panel of his radio, replacing it with a map of the United States. He then installed tiny red light bulbs at each city location, and manipulated the innards of his radio set so that when KDKA was being received, for example, the city of Pittsburgh's red light would brighten.

After perfecting his invention, the Elliot boy fell into the mare's nest of the U.S. Patent Office and its lawyers, who even back in those simpler days spent considerable effort at discouraging Americans from inventing things. Month after month went by while the Elliot boy dickered with Powel Crosley, who appeared eager to add the city-finding map to some of his radio models as soon as a patent was granted. Just about the time that preparations were underway to put the Elliot map radio set into production, networks of stations began forming around the country. Most stations rapidly joined the networks, and almost every night the same broadcasts were beaming out from dozens of cities. People now began talking about the different programs. No longer did it matter which city a set was receiving. And so the Elliot boy lost his chance to become a millionaire. This had little effect on his peers, however. We continued to think of him as a mechanical genius.

Then there were the Powell brothers. Dick was by this time out of his teens and no longer one of the gang. About all we saw of him was when he sang in church or in one of the downtown theaters. Almost before we realized it, he was singing in nightclubs in the East, and eventually he was making movies in Hollywood—musicals such as *42nd Street*.

His teenaged younger brother, Luther, was one of the gang, and he took Dick's sudden fame in his stride. After completing a movie, Dick would send Luther some of the suits he had worn during the filming. This, of course, attracted girls from all around the area, and when members of the gang would gather at the neighborhood drugstore for root beers, pretty girls would suddenly appear to see what suit Luther was wearing. As most of us were rapidly reaching the age when girls interested us, we viewed Luther as a sort of honey pot to attract them. As far as he was concerned, however, the movie clothes were nothing special, just an amusing part of growing up during the early years of talking pictures.

The change from silent to talking pictures brought unemployment to one of the prettiest girls in our neighborhood. She was a few years older than the members of the gang, but we all had crushes on her because she treated us as if we were sophisticates like we thought she was. She played the giant organ in one of the first-run theaters on Main Street, and in those latter days of the silent films, the movie companies provided theaters with cue sheets and elaborate musical scores that would arrive a few days before a particular film. The young organist usually brought the sheets home so that she could practice playing them on her piano, and sometimes when we heard her playing we would go and sit in her porch swing or on the front steps and listen. If the weather was rainy or cold, she might invite us inside with a stern command to sit quietly while she practiced.

One day she showed us a musical score, pointing out the cue words for scenes in the movie, and laughingly told us that much of the music was used over and over again—excerpts from Bizet's *Carmen*, the *William Tell* Overture, a good lot of Scott Joplin's ragtime pieces for two-reel comedies, and bits from Dvorak's *New World* whenever Indians appeared in Westerns. She said that as a result of playing movie scores, she was more interested in classical music than she had been before becoming a theater organist.

The talkies came in gradually, theater by theater. Her theater, after the change, retained her for a while to play the giant organ at the beginning of each showing because audiences had become accustomed to the powerful music with sound effects of bells, whistles, clangs, and thrums that she brought out of that wonderful instrument. Eventually, however, the organ concerts were discontinued, and when I left Little Rock she was teaching piano lessons to the young.

The freight trains we rode on belonged to the late lamented Chicago, Rock Island & Pacific, and every Saturday morning a long line of Rock Island cars would crawl out of the switching yard to the south bank of the Arkansas River and turn west toward Tucumcari, New

Mexico, gradually gathering an exhilarating speed. We preferred to ride in high-sided coal cars because they were easy to get in and out of, and were safer than flatcars, especially if a dozen or so teenagers were monkeying about and showing off on them.

After traveling several miles along the river, the train would begin to slow and eventually come to a stop. Alongside a tall tank, the steam locomotive would begin to take on water, and we would quickly drop off the train. At this point we were a dozen or so miles from Schiller Street, with no way of returning by train. Our *modus operandi* was to scale a steep rocky bluff and then walk for two or three miles through a pine woods to Forest Park, where there was an outdoor swimming pool and various other devices for entertainment. The amusement park was also the end of a trolley line. From there we could ride all the way home for five cents. Our outing was an exciting and economical but hazardous way to spend a Saturday morning. Like a secret society, we guarded this activity from our elders, as well as from younger boys and from girls of any age in the neighborhood.

These expeditions came to an abrupt and almost disastrous end one fine autumn Saturday. The sky was bright blue, the air fresh and cold enough for heavy sweaters. The only portent of what lay ahead was a pestiferous railroad bull who drove us off an empty coal car while the train was still standing. With rich profanity he then ordered us away from the switching tracks. We had rarely been troubled by these railroad detectives before, and had never been ordered away. We regrouped up the slope above the tracks and decided to wait until the train started moving, when each of us would run down and hop a separate car. We would then climb to the tops and walk to the coal car we had been chased out of.

The train moved very slowly at first, and we accomplished our objective with no mishaps. Because we had outwitted the yard bull, we all felt particularly jubilant. This merry mood, however, was soon shattered.

After the train passed a familiar sand shoal in the river, we started moving toward the ladder at the end of the coal car to make a hasty exit as soon as the locomotive stopped at the water tank ahead. Because the tracks ran very close to a rocky bluff, we always unloaded on the river side, which was open slope.

The train, however, was not slowing. Without warning, the cars surged forward, the way water will sometimes spurt suddenly out of a slow-running faucet. Around a curve ahead, we could see black smoke swirling out of the locomotive's stack as it swept past the water tank, gathering speed. Moments later we passed the water tank.

"Bail out!" somebody yelled, and off the ladder we went, one at a time. I remember striking the ground and rolling until a shoulder banged painfully against a large stone. I stood up slowly, gasping for breath and looking both ways along the track. The place where we jumped was a sharp-sloped grade that ran down toward a line of willows along the river. Frost-browned high grass covered the ground with numerous menacing stones scattered half-concealed through it. For a hundred yards lay a dozen teenagers, looking as if they had been mowed down by a machine gun. Gradually a few of us began rising to our feet, while others sat up to look around wonderingly at the others.

The train's caboose rattled by, a brakeman in its cupola looking back to laugh at us. We gathered closer together, some of us limping, some rubbing various parts of our bruised bodies. I think everyone hit at least one stone. One boy, whose nickname was Sleepy, still sat a few yards away, grasping his legs below his knees and sobbing audibly.

We examined each other, surprised that there was so little blood. Our sweaters and coats had protected our skin. We began laughing nervously and chattered about missing a trip to Tucumcari, New Mexico. We began discovering scratches on hands and faces and a few torn sweaters and pants.

We looked uneasily at Sleepy, waiting impatiently for him to get up and join us. But he still sat there staring at the river. We all went over to him. The knees of his trousers were ripped across and his kneecaps were without skin and covered with seeping blood. We helped him to his feet, and he tried to walk, moaning at every step.

Because the train had failed to stop at the water tank, we had a longer distance than usual to walk, and much of this was over a railroad track ballasted with sharp-edged gravel. It soon became

quite obvious that the wounded Sleepy would have to be carried
much of the way.

The Hollis brothers and Luther Powell were the most muscular
members of the group, and they did much of the carrying. But when
we started up the steep climb to the pine woods all of us took turns
at bearing him on our backs or lifting him up the pathway with
crossed arms, Boy Scout style.

Around noontime we reached the end of the trolley line. To
the little group of people waiting there we must have looked like a
band of pillagers who had been driven away by our intended victims.
They stared at our ripped clothing, our scratched hands and faces,
and the occasional smears of blood we'd received from Sleepy's
oozing knees while portaging him up the bluff and through the
woods. A buxom silver-haired woman finally summoned the
courage to ask Sleepy what had happened to him. We had already
prepared an explanatory story for the benefit of our elders, and
Sleepy responded correctly. We had been out to Pinnacle, a small
mountain a few miles beyond the place where we had leaped off the
freight train. While trying to descend on the steep side of Pinnacle,
Sleepy had lost his footing and fallen upon a ledge, and then several
of us had skinned and bruised ourselves while rescuing him.

How successful our tale was with the people at the trolley stop
we never knew, but Sleepy later told us that the doctor who came
to dress his wounded legs did not believe a word of it. At any rate,
we discontinued the Saturday morning freight train rides and turned
to other activities.

Most of the freight-train riders were also members of the annual
Halloween marauders, whose main objective was to turn on the fire
alarm at the corner of Sixteenth and Schiller streets precisely at
midnight of Allhallows Eve. This was a custom that had originated
long before my Criner cousins and I had come to Little Rock, but
we felt it our duty to participate. In those days, red fire-alarm boxes
were scattered around the city. All that was necessary to summon a
fire truck was to break a thin piece of glass with a small metal stick
that hung on a chain from the box. This caused a signal receiver in
the Little Rock fire station to sound an alarm and indicate the

location of the box. In these modern lawless days, no such system could exist; every box in the city would be vandalized in one night. But in those almost crime-free times, when people never bothered to lock the doors of their houses, no one would have dreamed of touching a fire-alarm box unless there was a fire. Except at Sixteenth and Schiller streets on Halloween at midnight.

On the morning of the last Little Rock Halloween that I had a hand in—October 31, 1926—one of the newspapers noted on its front page that the weather for Allhallows Eve would be clear and mild, and that the city police department would be at full strength. In addition, Fire Chief Burns announced that his men and equipment were prepared to respond to all calls, but he cautioned celebrants against overlarge bonfires of leaves or other combustible materials. The last sentence in the news item stated that city authorities were determined to prevent the annual false alarm from the box at Sixteenth and Schiller. Two plainclothes detectives would be on duty in the area all evening.

Before noon every member of the Halloween marauders had either read or been told about this news item. What a challenge this would be!

As Halloween fell on a Saturday that year and we no longer hopped freight trains, we had an entire day to make preparations. On a back lot between Schiller and Park, where we usually played games of shinny, several of us met from time to time during the morning to present ideas for pranks and to plan a stratagem to outwit the two plainclothes detectives we had been warned about.

At the corner of Sixteenth and Park, opposite the neighborhood drugstore, was an abandoned building that had once housed a small grocery store. Yellow paint peeled from its graying boards, and no window had escaped some form of breakage. Our master planners decided that the rear of this ghost building would be our operations headquarters, it being only a block from our main objective, the fire-alarm box.

During the afternoon we assembled a collection of stones about the size of baseballs and placed them in high grass about twenty yards from the rear of the building. One of the Hollis boys brought a dozen or so rotting eggplants that he had been storing up and concealed them close by the stones. After dark he planned to lob these soft vegetables through the open windows of passing trolley cars.

We then met to select the person who would turn on the alarm. We voted my cousin Joe the honor after a few test races in which he beat out his competitors. We laid out an escape route from the alarm box though the side yard of the corner house into the back lot, along which he must speed to the rear door of his house and into bed. Along the route we designated two or three hiding places in sheds and behind thick shrubbery in the event of an emergency.

As soon as darkness fell, we were out on the streets, slipping quietly onto porches to unhook swings and carry them into yards, upend porch furniture, write messages with soap on a few windows, tape doorbells so they would ring continually, and switch flower-pots from one porch to another. At the corner where streetcars turned down Sixteenth Street from Park, we took turns jerking trolley arms off the overhead wires so that the conductors had to come outside and replace them. As the cars started up again, the Hollis boy would try to lob a rotten eggplant through a window. On his last attempt he would have been caught in the act had not the trolley shielded him from view of the two plainclothes detectives coming out of the drugstore. Walter Reiman, who had worked part-time at City Hall, spotted them immediately and quickly passed the word.

With airs of innocence we entered the drugstore and lined up at the marble soda fountain for root beers all around. One of the plainclothesmen followed us in, pretending to be interested in buying a cigar. Some of us began chattering about an imaginary Halloween party we supposedly had been invited to attend.

The plainclothesman lit his cigar and went outside. We decided to split into two groups and head in opposite directions, circle the area, and rejoin at the ghost building. I was in the group that turned down Sixteenth Street, all of us quite aware that one detective was following us. Quick glances to the rear told us that he had stopped opposite the fire-alarm box and had seated himself on a low brick wall. We continued down the sloping street, one or two boys darting up on porches to seize a chair or anything loose and carry it to the sidewalk.

I can't recall who it was that crept silently upon the front porch of my favorite English teacher, Miss Dorothy Yarnell, tiptoeing back down the steps with a large potted geranium. I'm certain he meant to deposit the geranium on the sidewalk, but at that moment a trolley came rocketing toward us. Without missing a beat, the prankster strode out to the trolley track, placed the flowerpot at center, and started at a trot toward Battery Street. I badly wanted to rescue that flowerpot because I had a schoolboy crush on Miss Dorothy Yarnell. She epitomized all the beauty of the English language that she bade us read and write each day, and I was a slave of printed words. But there was no time for a rescue. As I fled shamefully with the others to turn onto Battery, I heard the crash of the disintegrating flowerpot and the shriek of braked trolley wheels. Then we were off again, dashing through the night to more distant neighborhoods. Off and on through the late evening we teased the detectives merely by strolling slowly past the fire-alarm box. This made them very suspicious, very fidgety.

Midnight seemed a long time coming. Finally Jud Routh's wristwatch told us to gather at the ghost building and prepare to divide and conquer our two adversaries. At about ten minutes to midnight, cousin Joe concealed himself behind the hedges overlooking the fire-alarm box. From careful reconnaissances we knew that one of the detectives was in a car about half a block down Schiller. The other one had resumed his position on the brick wall across Sixteenth Street.

At about five minutes to midnight, we quietly lined up in front of the row of stones we had placed in high grass near the abandoned building. Jud Routh, being the only one of us with a watch, gave the signal to start hurling stones at the already broken glass windows. To our ears, the assault sounded like a crashing artillery barrage. A second wave brought the first detective off his brick wall and on a fast trot toward the building. Along the street the alarmed citizenry began turning on their porch lights. We were all scattering like a herd of startled deer just as the second detective turned his car tentatively around the corner at Schiller in a move to aid his companion.

Every one of us had a planned route of escape, and in a matter of minutes we were all in our beds. Cousin Joe, with the enemy outflanked, had a clear field down Schiller to his front door and he beat most of us into bed. Moments later the howl of a fire engine siren frazzled the peaceful night, and we all lay laughing in our beds, listening to the throbbing of the fire engine motors and the shouts of firemen resigned to responding to their annual Halloween call from Sixteenth and Schiller streets.

Next day, the newspapers published brief reports of our victory. That would be my last Halloween of pranks until I became an adult, and by that time the wicked deeds that we and many other teenagers committed across America had led society to defend itself by inventing the abominable custom of Trick or Treat. I'm very sorry for whatever small part I may have had in that.

I did not find Little Rock High School very interesting until I discovered that it offered courses in printing. At the earliest opportunity I enrolled in one of Mr. John Nolan's classes, eventually going through the whole lot of them. Sometimes I was irked by Mr. Nolan's unrelenting insistence that everything had to be as perfect as I could make it—the adjustment of space in the design of display ads, the proper choices of type faces, the setting of intricate material on that now extinct machine, the Linotype, the impressions of inked type upon paper—not too heavy, not too light.

I suppose the only persons from whom I learned anything worthwhile as a youth were those who believed in excellence. They insisted that if you could not excel, at least you must try to excel. And so, John Nolan made me into a fair printer, ready upon graduation from high school to enter the trade as an apprentice.

Finding jobs in those days was no easier than it is now; probably it was more difficult. As there were no jobs locally for an eighteen-year-old printer, I wrote to several small-town newspapers around the state. Miraculously, an angel responded.

CHAPTER FOUR

Teenaged Printer and Fledgling Journalist

THE ANGEL WHO GAVE ME MY FIRST JOB as a printer was Mr. Tom Newman of the Harrison *Daily Times* in Boone County, Arkansas. He could employ me for a month, he wrote, in the weeks before Christmas. I should report at the earliest possible date, he emphasized, as the Christmas card printing season was already beginning.

My family was aghast when they consulted a map and found that Harrison was a town buried so deep in the Ozark Mountains that no one we knew had ever been there or had even heard of the place. The only way to get to Harrison was by way of the Missouri & North Arkansas, which we were informed was the railroad that Thomas W. Jackson had used as the model for his scurrilous joke book, *On a Slow Train Through Arkansaw.* A neighbor told us that people who lived along the M.&N.A. always referred to it as the May Never Arrive, and that it was notorious for washed-out bridges, loose rails, and frequent accidents. I was warned not to go.

Nevertheless, early one chilly November morning I boarded the Missouri Pacific and rode up to Kensett, where there was a junction with the M.&N.A. When I arrived at Kensett, I had the feeling that I was Sherwood Anderson's George Willard leaving Winesburg, Ohio. To celebrate this perception of literary manhood, I purchased a cheap cigar at a drugstore near the station and smoked it until dizziness and nausea forced me to cast it away.

The Harrison-bound train finally arrived at Kensett about two hours late, drawn by a clanking, hissing, wheezing steam locomotive. It was only after I boarded that the realization suddenly struck me that I was bound into the unknown, my only security being a

Courthouse Square, Harrison, early in the century (courtesy Steven Hanley)

Boone County Court House, Harrison. Ark.

The Harrison Times building faced the Boone County Courthouse (courtesy Arkansas History Commission)

letter from the publisher of the Harrison *Times* who signed himself *Thomas Newman, Esq.* I had read his letter a hundred times and knew every word of it by heart.

We were soon passing through towns whose names I had never heard before—Mount Pisgah, Letona, Pangburn, Snell, Higdon, Edgemont—each being impressed upon my memory because I have forever been fascinated by place-names. As we began to move up into the hill country, a train butch in a shiny blue serge suit and hard-visored cap came through the car. I asked if he had any books, and he brought a basket of dime novels for me to make a selection. I chose *Jesse James and the Great Train Robbery* and became so involved in it that I forgot we were traveling through the very same country in which Jesse had actually practiced his banditry. I remember once or twice lifting my eyes from the pages to glance out the window. The train was climbing alongside a crooking stream which was alive with rapids and sparkling little waterfalls. Sometimes I could see the locomotive up ahead swinging in and out as it rounded curves, and sometimes the engine would be reflected in the creek below, creating an illusion of stream and train racing happily toward some pleasant destination.

When we reached Harrison, darkness had fallen. I felt lost and lonely there on the cinder platform in the still November night listening to the panting of the weary locomotive. All the other passengers who got off hurried away to familiar havens, but I had to search out a place to stay the night. I managed to find my way to the courthouse square (which when I recently saw it was almost the same as it was in the late 1920s). I found a hotel of sorts, above a drugstore, and the desk man eyed me suspiciously when I inscribed my name and Little Rock address. "Little Rock? What you doing so far from home, boy?"

"I'm here to work for the Harrison *Times,*" I said.

"Oh? The Newman brothers."

"Mr. Tom Newman," I explained.

"Yeah. And John. Tom hires and John fires, they say." He grinned at me and said the hotel room would be a dollar and a half in advance.

Next morning, very early, I was standing in front of the Harrison Times building, which also faced the courthouse square. The rickety door was locked. My view of the interior through the dingy windows was less than I had expected, but I was reassured by the faint whiffs of printer's ink which seeped from the door cracks. I wondered what that hotel man had meant by "Tom hires and John fires." It was cold, and I was shivering in my cheap mackinaw and wishing I was back home in Little Rock, when a boy about my age, his black hair greased down in the Rudolph Valentino fashion of that time, came swinging off the courthouse lawn. He was reaching for a key when he noticed me. "You waiting for somebody?" he asked.

When I said I wanted to see Mr. Tom Newman, he replied that he would be in about seven. He opened the door and invited me inside. I told him who I was, where I was from, and why I was there. His name was Bill Farley, and he was a printer himself, acting as makeup man and pressman for the daily *Times*. I followed him through the untidy office into the printing area, which was crowded with type racks, stone tables for making up pages, two job presses, and a ponderous old hand-fed newspaper press. There were also two Linotypes; one was in fairly good condition, but the other one must have been the first off Mergenthaler's production line. I was looking them over when Bill Farley remarked that he could do everything in a print shop except run a Linotype. "John never taught me that," he explained.

"Who's John?" I asked.

Farley said that John was Tom's younger brother and that he ran the Number One Linotype. "Tom *thinks* he's the boss," he added, "but John *is* the boss. Tom is so chicken-hearted he'll hire anybody who asks for a job. Then when the shop gets overcrowded and the payroll too big, John fires everybody but me and the Number Two Linotyper, and the girl who writes the local news. That's all we need to get out an eight-page daily."

About this time a man of around forty appeared suddenly, his eyes blinking at me with mild surprise. He was Tom Newman. I introduced myself; he smiled uncertainly and invited me into his cubbyhole of an office. His desk and visitor's chair were piled high with newspapers, some of them cut into strips by his clipping shears. He emptied the chair by dumping the papers on the floor and motioned me to sit down. I was soon to learn that Tom spent much of his time cutting items from other Ozark newspapers, each day passing a sheaf of clippings on to John, who chose any he felt appropriate for the Harrison *Times*. The *Times* also subscribed to the Associated Press pony service, which furnished considerable feature material and gave the paper the right to use any AP news published in other papers. In those days, the teletype had not yet been introduced. A few minutes before press time each day, John would make a phone call to Little Rock and the AP man would read him five minutes of late bulletins, which were hastily set into type and locked into the front page.

While I was sitting there with Tom, I began to realize that my name had meant nothing to him and he was evidently wondering why I was there. I explained that I was the young man from Little Rock he had hired by mail to print Christmas cards.

He smiled vaguely and withdrew a cardboard box from under his desk. "We already have one order," he said. "Mr. and Mrs. King. They always want their names imprinted on their cards. You can do them this morning."

He called Bill Farley and told him to show me to one of the job presses. Neither press looked as if it had been recently used. I cleaned up the better one, set Mr. and Mrs. King's names in something like fourteen-point Gothic, proofed it, locked it into a chase, inked the circular plate, and carefully went through all the steps of make-ready that I had learned in school.

After a few trials and errors, I got a perfect impression, and then started the motor. I was so absorbed in my first professional printing job that I was scarcely aware of the clicking Linotypes behind me, but when I walked back to Tom Newman's office to report that the cards were all finished I passed the two machines. At the Number Two Linotype, which as I said was probably the first ever produced by Mergenthaler, I saw a large man with a purple-veined nose engaged in what appeared to be a death struggle with the machine. Type matrices and bits of hot metal were flying in all directions, and he was alternately cursing and reading his copy aloud. The only name I ever knew him by was Buck. At the Number One Linotype, a plump man who slightly resembled Tom Newman was smoking a cigarette in a long holder—like the one that Franklin Roosevelt used. He lifted his eyebrows as I passed but continued setting type.

Tom was absorbed in clipping newspapers and seemed to have difficulty in remembering who I was. I showed him one of the Christmas cards and informed him that the others were laid out to dry. "Very good," he said, "except you should have used Old English type for Christmas."

"Nope," a positive voice interrupted from the door of the cubbyhole. "Nope. Gothic's better. Who the hell can read Old English?"

Tom stammered out his brother's name. "John," he said and introduced me.

John glanced resentfully in my direction and inserted a fresh cigarette in his long holder. He reminded Tom that they had promised Fritz Herder that he could print their cards. Fritz, as I discovered later, was a German who had drifted into town and whom Tom had already hired to do job printing when it was needed. "Oh, we can give Fritz another batch of cards," Tom replied.

"But we don't have any more orders," John said.

"Well, we need some cards ourselves, goodwill cards to send to our advertisers," Tom said. "Fritz can print them."

"Oh, all right," John said, and glanced at me again. "What're you going to put this boy to doing now, Tom?"

"You don't have anything for him?"

"Nope."

Tom said he would find something for me to do. After John ducked out of the office and returned to his Linotype, Tom fumbled around in the clutter on his desk and found a folder that had samples of Christmas cards laid in. He looked at me and said: "Why don't you just walk around the square with these samples and show them to the merchants and let them pick out some for us to print for them?"

Never before in my life had I ever tried to sell anything like this. I was so frightened I could scarcely explain to the prospective customers what I was selling, but after receiving two or three small orders, I loosened up a bit. The trick, I found, was to remark with some exaggeration that all the other businessmen were ordering cards, and now, sir, how many would you like to have? By noontime I had sold a couple of dozen orders.

I got back to the newspaper office as Tom and John were leaving for lunch. John looked over my order list with skepticism, but he appeared to be impressed, especially with one sale I'd made, to the owner of a furniture store. "Why, he hasn't bought an ad from us in twenty years," John said. He handed the sales folder back to me. "The only catch is that we don't have any of these cards in stock, and we'd never be able to get them in here from St. Louis in time to print before Christmas."

Tom spoke up and said he'd go to the dime store on the way back from lunch and buy up some cards from them. "It won't matter if they are not exactly the same as those in the folder," he said.

John shook his head. "At dime store retail prices we'd lose money," he said.

"Goodwill, John, goodwill," Tom insisted. "Maybe the dime store will take a page ad for Christmas."

John, however, managed to obtain a supply of cards at wholesale from a friend at one of the drugstores. He then ran a display ad in the *Times* that produced several orders for name imprints from readers of the paper. For the next several days Fritz Herder, the German tramp printer, and I had plenty of Christmas cards to print. Meanwhile, Tom had hired a couple of schoolboys who had asked for jobs during the Christmas holidays to assist Fritz and me. We had to invent things for them to do. As Christmas drew near, Tom also hired a college student who had come home for the holidays and assigned him to assist Bill Farley, who needed no help either. The shop was getting crowded with excess employees.

About a week before Christmas I could see that we were coming to the end of the card orders. Just as I was beginning to like my job and the town of Harrison, my brief career appeared to be reaching a conclusion. But at least I would have forty or fifty dollars in my pocket, a goodly amount of money in those lean times.

One morning I went into Tom's office and asked him what day would be my last one. "Why not stay until we get out our Christmas issue?" he suggested. "Some of the ads will have to be hand-set."

So I worked until the big Christmas issue was printed. The next morning I went to the office to draw what I thought would be my last pay. John was the first of the brothers to come in. "I'm letting all the extra help go today," he said to me. "But Bill Farley tells me you can operate a Linotype." I told him that I could. "Well," he said, "Old Buck, who's been running the Number Two machine, decided to leave town last night. If you can set enough galleys of straight matter a day, the job is yours."

And so I was reprieved. But I soon discovered that Old Buck had not been putting on an act with that antediluvian Linotype. Almost every type matrix was bent or worn, the spacebands frequently stuck in the molding box, and hot metal would squirt out on my left leg. But somehow I managed to set enough slugs of straight matter each day to fill the columns of the *Times.*

One of the onerous jobs assigned to me was setting the country correspondence into type, weekly letters that came in from the mountain communities around Harrison. Most of the writers were women, and their letters chronicled the comings and goings of people in their neighborhoods—births, deaths, weddings, etc. This material was printed in the big weekly edition of the *Times,* which went mostly to those rural communities.

It was slow work setting country correspondence because much of it was written in pencil on cheap gray tablet paper supplied by the Harrison *Times.* The first of these letters that I saw were brought to me by John, who explained how I was to handle them. First, I was to watch for any item that might be newsworthy enough to excerpt and use in the daily edition of the newspaper. If I saw anything interesting I was to call it to John's attention. Second, whenever the spelling or grammar was very bad, I was to correct it—except in the case of letters from Bear Creek. The correspondent from Bear Creek had let the Newmans know in plain terms that her copy was to be set as she wrote it. One day when the Bear Creek correspondent came in to pick up a fresh supply of tablet paper and envelopes, I discovered why the Newmans left her copy alone. She was wearing a man's leather jacket with cartridge loops on the sides and I could see the brass heads of cartridges sticking out of them. Her checked skirt was not quite long enough to conceal a peg leg. I learned from John that the correspondent had lost her leg in a gun battle that developed during a family feud up near Bear Creek. From that day I always set her letters with great care, letting the participles dangle and the misspelled words stand as she wrote them.

My favorite correspondent was a Mrs. Livingston of the Compton community. She loved outrageous metaphors and similes. Instead of simply reporting that hog-killing time had brought fresh meat to the Thurman farm she would write: *The Thurmans have greasy chins this week.* In reporting weddings she would write a long paragraph describing the groom's appearance—his suit, shirt, necktie, socks, shoes, and haircut—and then add offhandedly that the bride wore the traditional white.

One week in Mrs. Livingston's letter I noticed a possible news item for the daily and showed it to John: *Mr. Cole, who is staying at our house, has discovered a cave near Compton. He says it is the largest cave in the Ozarks.*

John was not impressed. "The Ozarks are full of caves," he said. "People are always discovering caves. Set it without a head and we'll stick it in the daily news bits."

The next week Mrs. Livingston had another report on Mr. Cole and his cave. About halfway down the page, sandwiched between a wedding and a burned barn, was this: *Mr. Cole has been gone for three days. It is feared he may be lost in the cave he discovered.*

John was busily setting slugs for a difficult full-page ad, and he was annoyed when I interrupted him. But his eyebrows and cigarette holder shot up when he read the two brief sentences. "*That* could be news," he said. Back in those days the story of Floyd Collins trapped in Sand Cave in Kentucky was still fresh in everybody's memory. John frowned a minute, and then said, "Call up Mrs. Livingston and see what's going on out there." The Compton community had only two or three telephones, however, and Mrs. Livingston was not one of the subscribers, but eventually a neighbor summoned her to a phone. Mrs. Livingston said she did not know any more than what she had written in her weekly correspondence. Mr. Cole was still missing. She promised to call the *Times* collect if anything new developed.

When I informed John that nothing was going on out at Compton, he was still struggling to finish the ad by press time. "I think we should notify the Associated Press anyway," he said. "How about you calling the AP? Their number is pasted on the phone. Just read off what Mrs. Livingston wrote and tell the man that's all we know."

I found it extremely exhilarating to be talking to a representative of the Associated Press, and next morning when the *Arkansas Gazette* ran a brief item on its front page about a man believed to be lost in a cave, I felt a sense of real power. I had helped make news that everybody in the state was reading. And I also noticed that either the AP man or a copy editor at the *Gazette* had provided the mysterious Mr. Cole with initials. He had become "A.B. Cole." Somehow I felt that I had helped create him.

About midmorning, a call came from the *Gazette,* wanting to know whether a search had begun yet for A.B. Cole. John insisted that I get on the phone. "It's your story," he said. "You handle it." All I could say was that we had no further information from Compton. The *Gazette* man was disappointed and refused to hang up until I promised to call him the minute we heard anything. That afternoon, one of the editors of a Memphis newspaper telephoned; he said they were printing the brief item about A.B. Cole. And he asked: "Shall we send a reporter to cover the search?" He wouldn't believe me when I told him that as far as we knew no search had yet begun.

The next morning the *Gazette* carried a small follow-up item in its back pages, stating that nothing further had been learned of the whereabouts of A.B. Cole. That afternoon a St. Louis paper called and said they wanted a full account of the A.B. Cole story, with photographs. I replied that there was nothing new, but that we would keep them informed.

By this time I had become obsessed with A.B. Cole, and I knew I would have to go to Compton and find out more about him and his cave. I talked with Bill Farley about it, and he immediately became enthusiastic. Neither of us had a car, but he assured me that we could hitchhike out there Sunday morning.

So early Sunday morning we were standing at the road fork outside Harrison that led to Compton. After we'd waited for what seemed like an hour, I insisted that we start walking. "But it's twenty miles to Compton," Farley protested. "Up and down the mountains."

"We can walk there before sundown," I said. "If A.B. Cole is lost in that cave, the world ought to know about it."

Farley thought I was crazy, but he was game. We had walked about a hundred yards when a car pulled up beside us. The occupants were a man and wife whom Farley knew, and they were going out near Compton to tend their ginseng plants. Ginseng growing on shady Ozark slopes was a fairly profitable undertaking. The dried roots were collected in Harrison for shipment to China, where high prices were paid for them in the belief that ginseng would restore lost virility and cure all ailments afflicting mankind.

The ginseng growers let us off in front of the Livingstons' white frame house, and we went up and knocked on the door. A rather pleasant-faced plumpish woman opened it. She was wearing what in that place and time would be described as a Sunday dress. I told her that I was a reporter for the Harrison *Times*.

She was impressed and immediately invited us in. "Are you boys really from the *Times?*" she asked. I told her we were.

"Are you Newman boys?"

"No ma'am," I said and introduced Farley, explaining that we worked for the Newmans. "I called you on the phone the other day," I explained. "About Mr. Cole."

"Oh, yes," she said, and stared at me. "Why, I thought I was talking to a grown man on that phone. I didn't know you was just a boy."

I told her we had come out to Compton to find out more about Mr. Cole and his cave.

"Mercy," she said, "it's dreadful thinking of that poor man lost in that cave forever."

"Well, isn't anybody doing anything about it?" I asked.

She replied that since what had happened to poor Floyd Collins nobody around Compton wanted to set foot in a cave.

I asked, "Doesn't Mr. Cole have any friends or relatives here?"

She said no, that he was from somewhere way up in Missouri. He'd come to Compton to buy oak timber for a stave company and had been boarding with the Livingstons. After he'd found the cave, he'd been more interested in exploring it than in buying timber.

About this time Mrs. Livingston's husband came in, and they took us across a hallway to show us Mr. Cole's room. There wasn't much to see—a tabletop covered with crystal rocks, a couple of lanterns on the floor. A blue suit and some muddy work clothing hung in a closet.

When I asked Mr. Livingston whether he didn't think a search party should be looking for Mr. Cole, he replied that no one knew for sure that he was in the cave. "Maybe he found another cave," he said, "and got lost in it. Lots of caves around in these hills." But he did agree to take Bill Farley and me to see the entrance to the cave. We carried along one of Mr. Cole's lanterns.

We had to walk for some distance across the hills, and along the way Mr. Livingston entertained us with horror tales about men lost in caves until their skeletons were found years afterward.

At the edge of the clump of blackjack oaks, he showed us a crevice about six feet long, which was almost concealed by an overhang of brown sedge grass. It resembled a half-opened mouth. We got down on our knees and peered into the blackness. There was just enough space for a man to crawl inside.

After several minutes of nervous joking, we lighted the lantern and took a look inside. The smooth walls were curved and wet. We could see a narrow ledge just below the entrance, and gathering our courage we crawled inside and dropped down on the ledge. That was as far as we went. We called out Mr. Cole's name as loudly as we could, and listened, but all we could hear were echoes. When we climbed back outside, Mr. Livingston did not appear to be surprised at our quick return. We went back to his house, had Sunday dinner with him and his wife, and listened to some more of his chilling cave anecdotes until the ginseng growers came by and took us back to Harrison.

That night I wrote the story of Mr. Cole and his cave. I brooded over my composition, dragged in every lurid adjective I'd ever heard of, and borrowed from the horror stories I'd heard from Mr. Livingston as well as what I could remember of the tales of Edgar Allan Poe. Next morning I was down at the newspaper office early so I could use the typewriter. I typed up one piece for the St. Louis paper that had asked for a feature story, and a similar one for the *Arkansas Gazette,* and got them off in the mail by special delivery before starting to work at the Linotype.

For the first time since becoming a printer, I did not enjoy setting type that day. It struck me as being a rather mundane occupation in comparison with the heavenly experience of putting words together *before* they were set into type. Also I was restless. I could hardly wait to see my creative journalism printed in the two newspapers that had been granted the privilege of receiving my compositions.

I fully expected Wednesday's edition of the *Gazette* to have my cave story headlined on the front page, but it wasn't there. Far over in the back of the paper was a one-paragraph item stating that A.B. Cole, the missing man of Compton, still had not been found. When the St. Louis paper arrived, I searched it carefully, but there was nothing, not even a line. I was crushed.

A day or so later, the usual weekly Compton letter arrived from Mrs. Livingston. Evidently the visit Bill Farley and I had made to her house on Sunday was the event of the week. *Two young newspaper reporters from the Harrison* Times, was her opening line. Farther down was another item dropped in as casually as a mention of the weather. I couldn't believe what I was reading. I looked around for John to tell him about it, but he had gone out somewhere. Not long afterward, John returned accompanied by a well-dressed stranger carrying a briefcase.

Waving his cigarette holder in my direction, John said to the stranger: "Here's your young correspondent." He then explained to me: "This is Mr. Williams from St. Louis. His paper sent him here to do a piece on that man in the cave. I told him you know more about it than anybody else."

The St. Louis reporter said: "Young man, that was quite a story you sent us. Not our style exactly, but it inspired my editor to send me down here to do some digging into the missing Mr. Cole."

I pushed my chair back from the Linotype and stood up to shake hands. My face was burning with embarrassment, and I couldn't say a word.

"I've hired a car to drive out to Compton," the St. Louis

reporter went on. "I wonder if you could give me the names of some people I might talk with out there."

"Well, sir," I stammered. "I don't think there's much use of your going out to Compton now."

"Why not?" he asked in a somewhat startled voice.

I reached down and picked Mrs. Livingston's letter off the top of my file of country correspondence and pointed to a paragraph far down on the page. The reporter put on his glasses and began reading. "Good God," he cried.

"Let me see it," John said, reaching for the sheet of paper. He read the paragraph aloud: *"Mr. Cole who was feared lost in a cave has returned from Kansas City where he went for a visit."*

The reporter from St. Louis was peering at me through his glasses. "Boy," he said, "you sure brought me on a wild goose chase." He started laughing and then John joined in, but at that time I could not see anything funny about any part of it. I was convinced then that my brief career as a writer of words was ended forever and that I was destined to spend the rest of my life setting other people's words into type.

CHAPTER FIVE

How Not to Report A Tornado

As it usually does, fate intervened in my pursuit of the written word. While I was still at Harrison, it intervened in the form of a deadly natural occurrence. The event began one warm spring evening in the Boone County courthouse park. Four of us were there on one of the benches—Bill Farley and his girlfriend and I and a girl I would've liked to be my lady love but who was wearing the fraternity pin of a boy away at college in Fayetteville. We were idly debating whether we should wander across to the music store and ask permission to play some of the new piano rolls.

Soon after daylight turned to darkness, we began noticing violent lightning playing in the sky above the hills to the west and north. The flashes succeeded each other with such rapidity that the sky was kept in a state of continual illumination. Farley remarked that the storm was surely a gully-washer and probably would flood Crooked Creek, which sometimes flooded Harrison.

A half-hour or so later we learned that the storm was far more than a mere gully-washer. We were just on the point of leaving the park for the music store when a big truck with a fruit company's name on it rumbled into the square, the driver and several men in the back yelling at us. When the truck stopped, we walked closer to see what they wanted.

Green Forest, a town about twenty-five miles to the west, had been struck by a tornado and had sent out a call for help. Every man and boy in the courthouse park piled into the rear of the big fruit truck which immediately set off for Green Forest.

We found half of Green Forest devastated, the other half untouched. The truck stopped at the end of a tree-bordered street. Although the town had lost its electrical power, cars had been brought up and parked with motors running and headlights beaming so that we could see some of the destruction in the business section. In the fantastic manner of tornadoes, leaves and twigs had been sucked off the trees, leaving them bare as in winter but otherwise unharmed.

Those townspeople who had been least affected by the tornado were beginning to recover from the first shock of the disaster and had organized searching parties to bring in the injured and dead. A man with a lantern, which he swung nervously back and forth, directed us to a church that had been converted into a temporary hospital.

As we approached, a strong aroma of carbolic acid and other antiseptics enveloped us. On the wide steps of the church, illuminated by automobile headlights, a crowd of anxious-faced people milled about in confusion. From the open doorway came the cries and moans of injured children and adults.

The truck driver who had brought us from Harrison told us to wait on the steps. He then forced his way through the crowd and into the church. A minute or so later he returned. He said that the doctors inside wanted us to move out south of town as far as there was any evidence of tornado damage and search for victims.

For two or three blocks we walked in single file, winding our way around fallen trees, smashed cars, collapsed houses, and scattered furniture. Other searchers with lanterns and flashlights were delving carefully into wreckage that had hastily been passed over before.

At the edge of town was an open meadow. We spread out and walked across the wet grass toward the dark shape of a house that did not appear to be badly damaged. The sky was clearing, the stars shedding a milky light over the desolation. One by one we leaped a ditch running full with rainwater, and then we heard an eerie guttural moaning beyond an embankment just ahead of us. We climbed over the rise and found a heap of weathered timbers, the remains of a small shed. Those of us who had flashlights turned the beams on the splintered boards from where the sound seemed to be coming. We ran forward and pulled away the boards. Someone laughed with relief. "It's an old hog," he said.

Dozens of large splinters had been driven deep into the animal's back. "Anybody got a gun on him? We ought to put that hog out of its misery." No one had a gun.

We moved on toward the slightly damaged house, stumbling over tin cans of various sizes, hundreds of them, all labeled with bright red tomatoes. "The cannery," a man said. He stopped, pointing to one side. "It ought to be right over there." The cannery building was gone. Through the pale light we could see the rough outline of its foundations a hundred yards away. "It was a two-story building," the man said, wonderingly.

As we came up to the dwelling that we had been approaching, we saw for the first time that its windows and doors had been suctioned away by the vacuum of the tornado. The house had shifted slightly on its foundations but was still intact. A man inside must have heard us coming. He limped out on the slanted porch. "I thought nobody could find us," he said. "My wife is hurt and can't walk. I managed to get her on a cot, but I need help to carry her."

We took turns carrying the woman on the cot to the improvised hospital in the church. When we came to the church steps, I happened to be one of the carriers, and I had to go inside. Quilt pallets spread on the floor and the church benches were filled with injured people, a few sitting up, most lying down. The odors of antiseptics, blood, and human bodies were oppressive. I was glad to get out into the open air again.

Until dawn, our group continued making sweeps of the outer areas of the town, but we found no one else who needed help. Then we went to a big brick grocery store that had escaped the storm. Several young women, looking tired and sleepy, were serving coffee and sandwiches.

When we came out of the store into bright morning sunshine, Farley and I decided to explore the town by daylight. Along one block of dwellings the front walls of every house had been swept away in the freakish manner of tornadoes, leaving most of the furnishings inside untouched. Walking past these exposed habitations, we were reminded of displays in large furniture stores where chairs, sofas, and beds are arranged to simulate living rooms and bedrooms.

We walked on out to the edge of town to see by daylight the

remains of the canning factory. Along the way we picked up armloads of tomato cans and then put them down again because we did not know what to do with them.

A lanky young man, neatly dressed, was photographing the factory ruins. He turned around when he heard us approaching. He had a printed card stuck in his hatband that read: PRESS. He was from one of the towns west of Green Forest and had arrived that morning on the M.&N.A. mixed freight.

"We're from the Harrison *Times,*" I told him.

"Good," he said. "Maybe we can trade some information." He had not been able to find anyone in authority who could give him an estimate of the total property loss, the number of injured, and several other facts that he needed for his news story. He did know that seventeen people had been killed and the approximate time the storm had struck, two facts that I had not thought of as being essential until that moment. I finally decided to confess that we were printers, not reporters, but that we were going to try to take back as much information to the *Times* as we could.

We attached ourselves to the young reporter while he unknowingly gave me my first lesson in journalism. He led us back to the church where the temporary hospital was beginning to close down. The seriously injured were being transferred to hospitals in nearby towns; the slightly injured were being taken to the homes of relatives and friends. We then went to another church where the dead lay under blankets, seventeen of them, and we obtained permission to copy their names from a list. (I had to borrow a sheet of note paper from the reporter.)

Before that morning, I had never been in the presence of more than one dead person at a time—at funerals of relatives and friends—and I was shaken by the thought that on the previous evening those seventeen people had been fully alive and none could have believed that in a matter of seconds fate for no explainable reason would single each of them out for death.

After an hour or so of following the reporter around, Farley reminded me that we had better be getting back to our truck. Searching the town, we could find no trace of it and guessed that it must have returned to Harrison. For the first time, we realized that the day was moving on and that we should be in the Harrison *Times* shop setting type and making up pages for the daily edition. We tried frantically to find a Harrison-bound car, and then Farley remembered that an eastbound M.&N.A. passenger train should be coming through in a few minutes. We hurried over to the station and bought tickets. The lanky reporter was there, waiting for a westbound train. He was scribbling in his notebook. Occasionally he would stare intently at the ceiling and then dash off another line. After a while he closed his notebook and began pacing up and down in front of us, reciting to himself:

> *And all that beauty, all that wealth e'er gave,*
> *Awaits alike the inevitable hour:*
> *The paths of glory lead but to the grave.*

I was awed by this exhibition of literary scholarship. He was no doubt showing off before two green adolescents, but I admired him. "You went to college, didn't you?" I blurted out.

"Sure. Missouri. School of Journalism."

I wished I could have said that.

Our train arrived only fifteen minutes late and brought us into Harrison half an hour before press time. We ran all the way to the *Times* building. John was ramming slugs angrily through the Number One Linotype while Tom was fumbling around at the makeup table. "Y—y—you boys been over to Green Forest?" Tom asked.

We told him we had been. John got up from his chair, gave both of us hard looks, and said grumpily, "All we have on the tornado is a one-paragraph bulletin from Associated Press. Tom or I should have been at Green Forest getting a story, but we had to stay here and get the damn paper out."

I showed him the sheet of paper on which I'd scribbled notes about the tornado. "Maybe you can write a piece from this," I said.

"You write it," he retorted.

I started over to the typewriter.

"No time to type it," John said and pointed his cigarette holder at the Number Two Linotype. "The lead's hot. Write it as you set it. A whole column. You have less than half an hour."

Sitting there in front of that antiquated Linotype machine, I fought weariness and lack of sleep, feeling sorry for myself because John had asked me to do the impossible. There was no time to invent fancy phrases, to create magnificent figures of speech. I would have liked to insert that bit of poetry the lanky reporter had recited, but I could not remember the words and knew nothing else appropriate. Because I could not see the lines I was composing, I had to use short sentences and paragraphs.

I went over the deadline by two or three minutes. While I had been setting the type, John and Bill Farley had made up huge headlines that filled a considerable part of the front page. The remainder of the paper consisted of short news items with large headlines that John had set during the morning and a number of preset features that we always kept on hand for fillers.

As I was carrying my galley of type to the proof press, John swept it out of my hands and passed it to Farley to complete the front page. "If you proof it," John growled, "you'll want to correct something. No time for that. We're going to press."

For that reason, my tornado story had several typographical errors, only one of which was embarrassing. The "white-faced crowd" that I described standing on the church steps came out "white-faced crow," resulting in some smart-aleck remarks from my peers.

CHAPTER SIX

Encounter With the Newton County Law

NEITHER OF THE NEWMAN BROTHERS ever told me whether or not they liked what I had done with the Green Forest tornado story, but a few days later they sent me to report an automobile accident, and then a shooting in the hill country, after which followed a progression of other violent incidents. The local reporter for the *Times*, an earnest young woman, disliked violence, and there seemed to be a considerable amount of that in Boone County. Soon I was spending two or three hours a day writing blood-and-guts stories that I frequently composed directly on the Linotype.

About this time, Tom hired Asa Gurdy, a wild-looking mountain boy from around Jasper. Asa had spent the twenty years of his life in Newton County, the only county in Arkansas that never had a railroad cross its borders. He had seen pictures of locomotives, and upon learning that locomotives passed through Harrison, he walked about thirty rugged miles from his home for the single purpose of seeing one with his own eyes.

After keenly enjoying the sensory experiences of seeing, hearing, smelling, and touching a locomotive, Asa applied for a job with the Missouri & North Arkansas Railroad. The railroad had nothing for him, but Asa resolved to remain where he could enjoy watching the trains every day. In his necessary quest for employment, some anonymous person pointed him to the soft-hearted Tom Newman. As Asa could barely read and write, the only job he was suited for with the *Times* was that of janitor.

He enjoyed being janitor, and he was clever enough to spread about an hour's worth of cleaning and sweeping across an eight-hour day. He spent a lot of time watching me operate the Linotype machine or hanging over Bill Farley's shoulder while Farley made up the newspaper pages and adjusted the big printing press. Farley and I were always relieved when a locomotive whistle sounded, because Asa would hurry off to the station, returning after an hour or so with his oft-repeated description: "H'it was a-breathin' thar like a big mare after a hard plow."

Neither Bill Farley nor I was yet twenty, but we had a sort of pact to become wandering printers. In those days, to obtain printing jobs in most cities, a union card was required, therefore our first goal was to get into the union. We were hopeful that eventually Tom would hire some people who could handle our jobs temporarily while we journeyed to Little Rock to make application to the Typographical Union.

Asa Gurdy was of no use to us in this matter, of course, and neither was his older brother Gobel, who arrived from Jasper one day in search of Asa. Gobel looked even wilder than Asa, and his hulking, ape-like body was twice as big. He was wearing a greasy old cap with the brand name of a now-extinct motor oil across its front. His hay-colored hair bushed out around the edges of the cap. His face was triangle-shaped—a massive forehead, long hatchet nose, harrow teeth, and a receding chin. His eyes, which were a weird shade of blue, had no expression whatsoever. Asa took him in to meet Tom, and Gobel frightened Tom into hiring him without his even asking for a job. Because there was no work for an assistant janitor, Tom out of desperation made Gobel an advertising salesman, as he had once done to me with Christmas cards.

Easter was nearing, so Tom presented Gobel with a two-page mock-up of about twenty advertising spaces with pictures of rabbits, Easter eggs, chicks, and religious symbols. Gobel was to sell these spaces to merchants in the Harrison business section. He went off into the town square, whistling through his harrow teeth, his motor-oil cap pushed back over his coarse hair, his lunatic's eyes staring down every passerby.

About fifteen minutes after his departure, the telephone began ringing in Tom's office. Businessmen were calling to complain that some back-country moonshiner was trying to shake them down for cash for ads before they were even published. Tom told them calmly that it was not necessary to pay in advance, but some had already done so, unwillingly and fearfully.

Not long after that, a barber whose shop was nearby burst into the front office, his face red with anger. "Who the hell is that lunkhead you sent to sell me an Easter ad? At first I thought it was some kind of joke you boys were pulling. Then that rascal reached into my cash drawer because I wouldn't hand him the money myself. I've never had an ad in the *Times*, and I don't want any Easter ad this year or ever!"

Tom, with John's assistance, finally soothed the barber's feelings and returned the money that Gobel had taken from his cash drawer. Then the Newman brothers hurried out on the square to call off their advertising man.

All three returned together, Gobel quite pleased with his success, Tom pretending to be pleased at the wad of money that Gobel turned over to him, and John saying nothing. To keep Gobel busy, Bill Farley showed him how to oil and ink the presses and clean dirty type. Farley had little success, however, in teaching him how to feed sheets into the big press.

For the next two or three weeks, the Gurdy brothers roamed the shop, piddling at this job or that. Any stranger coming in would have sworn they owned the place. But finally John could stand no more. One morning, he brought out his brown severance envelopes and fired three boys, including the Gurdy brothers. They refused to accept the fact until John told them to clear out.

"Ain't you satisfied with our work?" Gobel demanded.

"Your work's all right," John replied. "We just don't need you any longer."

"Why'd you pick on us?" Asa asked. He looked at me and then Farley. "You didn't lay off them two boys."

"We need them," John said curtly and switched on his Linotype motor.

"You're not a righteous man," Gobel declared. "The Lord'll put his wrath on you." He stood glaring at John with his strange blue eyes for a minute or so, then he and Asa picked up their lunch sacks and left.

About seven o'clock that evening, a passerby saw smoke curling from the cracks around the closed front door of the Harrison Times building and summoned the fire department. The firemen could have entered through the back door, which was never locked, but they smashed in jauntily through a big front window. The fire was confined to two metal containers—oily cleaning rags—but the fact that it was in two places left little doubt that the blazes were purposely set. And there was little doubt in our minds as to who were the miscreants that had put the wrath of the Lord upon us.

For the next three or four nights, Farley and I were given the duty of guarding the shop. Armed with a long-barreled six-shooter supplied by John, we slept atop a stack of newsprint. Eventually we learned from the sheriff that the Gurdy brothers had been sighted around Jasper, and life returned to normal at the Harrison *Times*.

About this time, two local boys who had been away at college informed Tom they would soon be looking for temporary jobs during their spring vacation. Tom, of course, hired both of them, and as one of them could operate a Linotype and the other the press, Farley and I decided this was an opportune time to take a few days' leave for a journey to Little Rock to apply for apprenticeship in the printers' union.

Originally we planned to travel by train to Little Rock, but as we made preparations, Farley presented the idea of pooling our railroad fares to buy a derelict Model-T Ford he had located in the rear of a repair shop. When we returned to Harrison, he said, we'd own a partnership car. I fell for the scheme.

We spent a weekend removing the tattered top, rotted seats, and most of the body from the chassis. We built a crude wooden front seat and installed a box on the rear to serve as a tool and luggage carrier. With the help of a friendly mechanic we got the motor started and tuned up. In a last hurried effort at beautification we painted the wheels a brilliant scarlet.

On the final day before departure, it seemed everyone in town was giving us advice about the best route to Little Rock. No paved highways ran in any direction from Harrison. We were warned against taking the southeast route because of spring washouts and ungraded gravel. The road to the south, we were told, was hilly and crooked, but the gravel had been graded most of the way and the unbridged streams were passable—unless sudden rains came. If we could manage to reach Russellville we'd connect with a paved highway that would take us all the way into Little Rock.

On a fine sunny morning, with Farley at the wheel, we headed south for Jasper, the gas tank full and a spare tire tube and patching in the toolbox. We forded Crooked Creek several times and finally came to our first bridge at the Buffalo River. As we were crossing on the rough planking we noticed two cars blocking the other end. Four men armed with rifles and shotguns were leaning against the cars. Just as we rolled off the bridge, one of the men raised a hand for us to stop.

Cradling his rifle in one arm, he approached us leisurely. "Where you boys headed for?" he asked.

"Little Rock," we both said.

"Where you from?"

"Harrison," Farley replied. "What's all the commotion?"

"Somebody robbed the Bank of Jasper last night," the man explained. "We been deputized to stop everything coming and going." He glanced at the luggage box on the rear, and added: "When you get t'other side of town, I'd roll up mighty slow if I was you, and act real polite. They'll search you for sure, going out of town."

We stopped at the only service station in Jasper and filled our steaming radiator. A man rode up on a mule, studying us with suspicion. He was so tall that his feet almost touched the ground beneath the mule. We said good morning to him and went on our way. A short distance out of town we sighted several cars parked in a semicircle and surrounded by about a dozen men and boys outfitted like a small army. As we approached, Farley cut our speed so slow that the old Model-T bucked in protest. A man wearing a star asked where we were from and where we were going.

"I need to search you," he added. We had to turn our pockets wrong-side-out and take off our shoes and socks. While he was feeling under our shirts for money belts, two men searched our car, removing boards from the front seat and taking our suitcases from the wooden box. While they went through our cases two others crawled under the car and examined it thoroughly. Although we could tell from their faces that they still considered us suspicious characters, the man with the star said we could go on our way.

As I was starting to hand-crank the motor, a pickup truck rattled alongside in a cloud of dust. The driver yelled out our names. I looked up, and there was Gobel Gurdy, showing his harrow teeth in a big grin. Sitting beside him was his brother Asa and a yellow coon dog.

"What're you and Farley doing way over here?" Gobel asked as he jumped out of the truck. "You robbed that bank, I reckon."

"We thought you and Asa did it," I said.

He pulled off his motor-oil cap and slapped it against his leg, laughing. "I bet old John Newman fired you both, didn't he?"

Farley told him we were going to Little Rock to join the printers' union.

He grinned, his weird blue eyes shifting to our Model-T. "Mighty fancy rig you boys got there. This pickup we driving belongs to Hawkins' sawmill. Mr. Hawkins sent us out to hunt the bank robbers."

Asa spoke up. "We going to catch them robbers and git us that ree-ward."

Gobel moved over to our car and rubbed a hand over the scarlet wooden spokes of the front wheel. "I like these fancy red wheels here. Wish I was going to Little Rock with you boys. Never been there."

"Climb on," Farley said, not meaning it. "Say, does this road take us all the way to Russellville?"

"I reckon," Gobel replied, and pointed south.

I cranked the motor, and the crowd, now viewing us with tolerance instead of suspicion, parted respectfully to make way for our Model-T.

As we jolted on southward the road became progressively worse, with potholes and deep ruts that set the car to bouncing. We were climbing much of the time and had to stop occasionally at creek fords to get water for the radiator. At the top of a high hill, while we waited for the radiator to stop boiling, we ate our luncheon sandwiches, and then I took over the wheel.

I had been driving only a short time when we came to a road fork. There was no highway sign, no house in sight, and no cars coming or going to tell us which route would take us to Russellville. We finally decided that the road to the right appeared to be the most used, and so off we went to the right. After a few minutes we could hear a car approaching fast from the rear. I glanced back and could barely see the hood of a pickup truck through our screen of dust. A horn blared. I looked back again, saw the pickup bearing down on us, and immediately turned our Model-T off on a grassy shoulder to let it pass.

As soon as the truck was ahead of us, it swerved to block the road, and came to an abrupt stop. Two men dropped off the rear bed, rifles at the ready. Two others jumped out of the cab, similarly armed. They were the Gurdy brothers and two companions.

"Git out with your hands up!" Gobel shouted.

We did as he ordered. Gobel and Asa sidled up, regarding us with sly smiles. "You sure fooled us mighty slick," Gobel said.

"What the hell have we done?" Farley cried angrily.

"You tell us," Asa retorted.

"Yeah, we believed you was going to Little Rock," Gobel said.

"We are," I insisted.

"Not now, you ain't." Gobel fixed his bluish eyes on me. "You're going right back into Jasper!"

"Almighty slick," Asa said. "Fooling us into thinking you was going to Little Rock. And then circling back for Huntsville."

"Yeah," Gobel added, "if we hadn't followed you you'd been in Oklahoma afore dark. Whar'd you hide the money? We want that ree-ward."

Well, we had taken the wrong road, but all our protests and solemn swearings of innocence availed us nothing. We had to subject ourselves to another search, and then were herded back to the roadblock where the man with the star took charge of us. With cars in front and behind us, rifle barrels jutting out of each vehicle, we drove caravan style into Jasper. The man with the star, who was the county sheriff, motioned with his rifle for us to turn down a narrow side street and into a rocky back yard.

As soon as I killed the motor, Gobel was at the sheriff's side, telling him not to forget that he and Asa were due the reward.

"Through that door," the sheriff ordered Farley and me.

Not until I stepped into the coolness of the gray stone building did I realize that it was the county jail. The interior consisted of a single cell of perpendicular iron bars and an office of about the same size. Seated on a hickory chair with his feet propped on a battered desk was the long-legged man we'd last seen riding a mule. He was the jailer.

"Well, I'm not a-tall surprised," he said when he saw Farley and me. "I kind of figured you boys for the robbery." He reached for the handcuffs suspended from nails on the walls.

"You won't need handcuffs," the sheriff told him.

Farley spoke up: "Sheriff Henry in Harrison is a good friend of my dad. If you telephone Mr. Henry, he'll tell you we're not bank robbers."

"You boys know we can't talk on the phone to Harrison," the jailer said, "because you cut the wires somewheres. Before or after you robbed our bank." He grinned as he opened a big canvas-covered book and dipped a pen in an inkwell. "What's the charge going to be, Harve?"

"Well, I don't know," the sheriff said. "Suspicion of robbing the Bank of Jasper, I reckon."

"That'll do it." He asked for our names, and then scratched the pen across the page, continuing to talk while he wrote. "You know, I've heard it said that Jesse James and the Younger boys used to pull that trick. They'd go into town and rob the bank and then so as not to be chased they'd hang around the place figuring they'd not be noticed in the excitement. Sometimes they'd even pretend to help in the trackdown."

Gobel and Asa, who were still in the office, resumed their demands for a reward.

"You'll get the reward after we find the money and convict these robbers," the sheriff said in a tone of exasperation.

A few minutes later we were locked up in the cell. The jailer gave us a checkerboard to pass the time. We sat there on the hard bench playing checkers through the afternoon. I've hated that game ever since. One by one and two by two the entire population of Jasper must have passed through the jail to view the captured bank robbers. We felt like animals in a zoo cage. Around dusk the jailer brought us some sardines, cheese, and soda crackers on tin plates.

"I'm going to lock the jail now," he said. "Deputies'll be guarding front and back all night, so no use you trying to escape."

"How about the telephone?" Farley asked. "Has it been fixed yet?"

"No, it's deader'n a dynamited fish. You boys ought not to have cut the wires."

No lights were in the jail, and after darkness fell there was nothing to do but lie on the hard benches and try to go to sleep. We talked about everything in the world except what had happened to us that day and tried to forget the iron bars and gray limestone surrounding us. We slept in fits and starts through what was the longest night I had endured in all the eighteen years of my life.

Even after the dim light of first dawn showed through the small barred windows, the time continued to drag until the long-legged jailer unlocked the outer door. He was whistling a mournful tune but had brought a tin can of warm coffee that he passed through the bars to us.

"Are you boys ready to tell us where you hid that bank money?" he asked with a chuckle.

We didn't feel like laughing back at him. We just shook our heads at the absurdity of the question.

"Try the telephone," Farley said. "If it's working I want to talk to my dad and ask him to get us a lawyer."

"Yeah, you'll need one today, I 'spect." The jailer walked to the telephone and picked up the receiver. "By God, it's working. I'll see if I can get the Boone County sheriff's office." He gave the operator a number and waited. We could hear faint clicks and hummings, and the mumblings of the jailer. Then his face broke into a grin. "Well, I'll be dog-danged," he said. "Up at Lead Hill. Well, I'll be dog-danged."

He hung up the receiver and walked across to our cell, carrying a long key which he inserted in the lock and then opened the heavy door. "Well, the joke's on us, boys. Just like I figured, the robbers went north toward Missouri. Two of Sheriff Henry's deputies caught 'em up at Lead Hill." He scratched his head. "Where was it you boys was heading for?"

"Little Rock," we said.

"Well, you can go on now."

He led the way to the rear door. "Your car's back here, ain't it? You boys drive careful and stay out of trouble."

We walked out into the rocky yard where we'd left the Model-T parked. The chassis of the car was still there, but all four of the shiny scarlet wheels were gone. It was like coming unexpectedly upon the mutilated body of a dear friend. I repressed a cry of grief and shock. Farley began raging profanely.

The jailer evidently was as surprised as we were. "That car of your'n is more'n a mite damified," he said.

"We want our wheels back," Farley shouted. "If you hadn't locked us up, we'd still have our wheels and be halfway to Little Rock."

"Now, hold on, son," the jailer protested. "I was only carrying out my duties. Gobel and Asa Gurdy, they are the ones to blame. If you don't believe me, come back inside and I'll show you my charge book. I got it writ down. Accusers Gobel and Asa Gurdy, so they would get the reward."

Farley looked at him with pure disgust. "Ah, to hell with the Gurdys," he said.

We never recovered our red wheels and we never reached Little Rock in the Model-T. For all I know, the car's rusting remains still rest there in the rocky yard behind the old Jasper jail.

CHAPTER SEVEN

Becoming an Old West Fanatic

SOME WEEKS AFTER OUR INCARCERATION in the Newton County jail at Jasper and the dismemberment of our Model-T Ford, Bill Farley rode a train down to Little Rock and was accepted into the printers' union. By that time, however, I had decided to change the direction of my life.

During that summer, a local boy of my age returned to Harrison from the state university and as he was a good Linotype operator, Tom gave him the part-time job of taking over the Number One machine while John was on vacation and filling in for me when I was working on an assignment. This boy's name was Eugene Wilson, and we would be friends for half a century. Through him that summer I met several other college students in the town. For me, it was an entirely new world. One Sunday afternoon I was invited to join a group of them for an outing to the Buffalo River. During this occasion I happened to mention casually that I hoped some day to become a professional newspaper writer. The students were soon arguing heatedly among themselves as to whether H.L. Mencken or Walter Lippman was the best working journalist.

As I had never heard of either of them, I felt entirely left out and terribly uninformed. The discussion led to other contemporary writers, and thanks to the Little Rock Public Library I could hold my own with Sherwood Anderson and John Dos Passos, but I knew nothing of several others the students had read in college. (Incidentally, writers were much more important to young people in the 1920s than now, as there were then no rock or country music stars and only a few famous athletes or movie stars—and most politicians were viewed as buffoons.) One of the boys whose family was well-to-do had been to Europe early in the summer and was very proud of having smuggled through U. S. customs an unexpurgated novel by D. H. Lawrence. Again I felt like an outsider because I knew nothing of the book or its author.

Largely because of my association with these students, I began reading magazines that I had paid little attention to before— *Scribner's, Dial, Mentor, Vanity Fair, Smart Set, Golden Book, American Mercury, Harpers, Atlantic*—many of the great periodicals of that age when American letters still flowered. Hemingway, Faulkner, and Fitzgerald were just beginning to come upon the scene; none of them was yet famous.

It was a wonderful summer for a teenager approaching twenty, with weekends in the mountains, swimming parties, and picnics with pretty Ozark girls. I fell in and out of love twice, and then suddenly I realized the summer was ending. The students were buying new clothes and preparing to leave for their various campuses.

One evening as I was walking a college girl home from a movie at the Lyric, she talking dreamily of returning to the university in a few more days, I came to an abrupt decision. The next morning I told the Newman brothers that I was leaving to go to college. They were accustomed to sudden departures of tramp printers. They wished me good luck, and Tom slipped an extra ten dollars into my last pay envelope.

Although I was never to return to the Harrison *Times,* I came to realize in later years the enormous debt I owed that little daily newspaper and the Newman brothers. The encouragement to write they gave me was never in spoken words but simply in the opening of the columns of their paper to an occasional half-baked effort from an inexperienced youth. Once in a while one or the other of the brothers would point out to me a better way to tell a news story, and from them I gradually learned, subconsciously perhaps, about clarity and conciseness. When I left their employment, they probably soon forgot me, but I have never forgotten Tom and John Newman for the parts they played in helping me learn the skills I would use for the remainder of my days.

I might never have been financially able to attend college had not my mother and Corinne moved from Little Rock to Conway so that

Corinne could enroll in the Arkansas State Teachers College. As the school then lacked sufficient dormitory space, many students paid for room and board in houses in the town. My mother rented a large house near the campus and opened it to young women students. After Corinne acquired a license and went off to teach, my mother invited me to come and help convert the house into a boarding place for male students.

As my friend Eugene Wilson at Harrison had been offered a night job setting type for the Conway *Log Cabin Democrat,* he transferred from the state university to the Teachers College and became one of the five students in my mother's boarding house.

Life as a college student in the 1920s is a commonplace subject; I will avoid the usual escapades, the courtings, the celebrations. It was my good fortune to be there at a time when that small college was blessed with several young professors just starting their careers in the humanities. They had come from good universities around the country, had not yet become bored with academia, and were eager to prove themselves.

From Constance Mitchell, a jolly and plump and always smiling member of the English Department I learned the beauty of good literature and the power of a well-structured sentence. From Ada Jane Harvey of the Foreign Language Department, an urbane woman who had spent some time in France, I learned that a knowledge of other languages is essential if one hopes to achieve fluency in the all-encompassing English language. From H.L. Minton of the Geography Department I learned about a broader world than the restricted one I had grown up in and acquired a deep fascination for historical maps.

Perhaps the college activities most useful to me were experiences on the college newspaper as a writer and editor, and the three years I worked as a student assistant in the college library. At that time and for many years afterward, writing was for me an avocation. There is far more printed matter in a library than in a newspaper office; I was born into the world of print, and my aim soon turned toward becoming a professional librarian.

The morning that I first set foot on the campus, I was greeted by a man who appeared to be no more than five or six years older than I. He was a good four inches shorter, but his head was massive, his hair close-cropped, his eyes very sharp and penetrating as he extended a hand and introduced himself in a gravelly voice as Professor Dean McBrien. The meeting was providential. McBrien was a professor of history from Nebraska, an enthusiastic student of western American history.

Dean McBrien more than any other mentor set me upon the course I was to take as a writer. He probably did not care very much for the historical novels I later published, but he could not help but like my way of writing history because I borrowed or stole the methods that he used in his classes to charm his students into listening attentively.

McBrien's view of history was that the past consisted of stories, fascinating incidents, woven around incisive biographies of the persons involved in the happenings. He liked little dashes of scandal—if they could be documented—and he insisted firmly that everything had to be authenticated from the available sources. He had saturated himself in the history of the American West. Before I met him, I was interested in the American West, but he converted me into a fanatic like himself.

Almost every summer during those years, he traveled across various parts of the West, usually with two students as companions. On two of these expeditions, I was privileged to be invited, and I learned far more than any classroom could offer.

McBrien preferred to travel in a Model-T Ford. Although the Model-A had replaced the Model-T, the latter was still available for a few dollars in various used conditions. By the time I was nineteen, I had owned or shared ownership in three different rattletrap Model-T's, and I had always accepted them as a part of the natural environment.

McBrien, however, made me see them for the remarkable machines they were, comparing them to the living, breathing steam locomotives that were beginning to pass from the railroads. When one cranked a Model-T into life, it would nudge forward like a friendly horse eager to be in motion. If the motor had been badly treated so that the spark lever had to be pushed down to make it start, the crank would kick, sometimes so hard the thrust would break a wrist. If a Model-T stopped running, a ten-year-old could repair it and drive it. If a tire blew out, the casing could be stuffed with dried grass or pine needles and put back on the road. If the radiator sprang a leak, a small bag of cornmeal poured inside would cure the ailment in five minutes. Because Model-T touring cars moved slowly, were open to the sun and wind, and afforded a perfect view of the landscape, Dean McBrien believed them superior to all other means of traversing the West.

On our journeys he never forced upon us his knowledge of events that had occurred in the places where we traveled, but if we gave him an opening—and we usually did—he would respond with one of his delightful little incidents, accompanied perhaps by an incisive biography, all laid out for us right where it happened.

When I hear that old adage about a good teacher needing only a log or a simple bench with the teacher at one end and the student at the other, I want to amend it to the front seat of a Model-T Ford with the student at the wheel and the teacher at his side, unlocking the past and relating it to present and future.

Perhaps because he was a Nebraskan, McBrien was fond of the Great Plains and refused to hurry across them, as so many travelers do, and from him I learned to admire the vast distances and enormous bowl of sky that would swirl above us with the passage of the slow-moving car. He must have read every overland diary and narrative then available, and would insist upon stopping for hours to examine places along the Oregon Trail, which we followed one summer.

These journeys and others that I later undertook on my own formed a basis for most of the books I would write. That time was more than half a century ago, a time not too distant from the years of cattle drives and the last Indian wars. We traveled mainly over unpaved roads across landscapes little changed from those of the nineteenth century. We had many small adventures, meeting inhabitants of small towns and Indians on reservations who remembered the great events of that nascent period of the West.

When a person who is cognizant of a recorded incident of history first comes upon the place where it occurred, the impact can have the force of an exhilarating electrical surge. I remember a

Brown (left) with Dean McBrien in Arizona, 1930

strange prickly sensation when, at twenty-one, I first saw the rude monument of stones beside the Bozeman Road in Wyoming, the marker of the Fetterman fight of 1866 near Fort Phil Kearny. This was a victory for the Plains Indians—Sioux, Cheyenne, and Arapaho—sometimes credited to the leadership of Red Cloud, the Oglala who demanded abandonment of forts along the Bozeman Road before he would sign the "lasting peace" treaty at Fort Laramie. Today, the Fetterman fight would loom much larger in the annals of the Indian wars had the Little Bighorn not overshadowed it ten years later. At first presence, I knew that something shattering had occurred there and around the site of the vanished Fort Phil Kearny, along the rim of deceptive ridges, to the brooding Bighorn range, misty and cloud-covered that day. The air was filled with courageous spirits of the past—red-man spirits, white-man spirits.

The Custer battlefield at the Little Bighorn struck me somewhat in the same way, but because we knew so much about it the place wasn't as compelling with myths as the hidden enigmas of Fort Phil Kearny. Thirty years later I thought I knew enough about what happened there to write the story of the forts and the Fetterman fight.

The sites of old Fort Wallace and Beecher Island would have been insignificant without the legends in our heads. Fort Wallace, in far western Kansas, had already vanished, leveled by time, when we visited the site. Wallace, the railhead that supplied the fort, was a ghost town. They had been booming centers of military action and commerce in the years immediately following the Civil War. Custer used Fort Wallace as a base in 1867. Lieutenant Frederick Beecher left there in 1868 to cross the Colorado Territory and meet his doom on an island in the Arickaree. When we found the place, Beecher Island had been erased by river currents, but the ghosts of Roman Nose and the dead frontier volunteers were still there.

In those useful years of searching, the most painful place we came upon was a mass grave with a few flowers struggling to live around it, in South Dakota, the Pine Ridge reservation. A monument bore the names of some Indians, but most of those buried there were unrecorded and unknown—men, women, and children, killed at Wounded Knee. That grave remained like the scar of a wound imprinted forever upon me.

The geographical place that has been the heart of the American West for me since the day Dean McBrien and I set eyes upon it in the late 1920s is Santa Fe. Here white Europeans commingled with American Indians before the Pilgrim fathers landed at Plymouth, before Virginia became a crown colony, long before a mission was founded on the soil that became San Francisco. Here the Pueblos were the first of the tribes to resist European assaults upon their religion and culture. They drove the Spaniards completely out of the territory and kept them out for several years. The American explorer, Zebulon Pike, was taken into custody here, and the published account of his experiences resulted in the coming of a flood of traders and the opening of the Santa Fe Trail. Here was engendered the Mexican War that brought the city into the United States. While Lew Wallace was territorial governor here, he wrote *Ben Hur* and dealt with such outlaws as Billy the Kid. On my first visit, I saw in the Palace of the Governors Lew Wallace's portable writing desk that fit handily over his knees, and I was quite impressed by the old Civil War general's craftsmanship.

In later years, my wife and I planned to settle down in retirement at Santa Fe, but the more we pondered the idea, the more we feared that the magic that attracted us could gradually fade away in the routines of daily living. Santa Fe is meant to be the objective of pilgrimages undertaken to honor an ageless doyenne, a queen mother of the American West, and it is a pity the entire urban area was not put off limits to developers fifty years ago.

Many years after my first visit to Santa Fe, I was there to attend a conference. The town was undergoing explosive population growth which would soon despoil its charm. The season was late spring, a time when the flagstoned plaza is a pleasant place to relax and watch enormous fluffy clouds build up in a pure blue sky. Sometimes by midday, separate clouds will darken and make little rain showers on the pine-clad Sangre de Cristo Mountains off to the north and west, but at this time of the year they seldom bring more than a sprinkle of drops to the plaza.

One morning a Tewa Indian with a bad limp came and sat beside me on one of the old filigreed cast-iron benches. After we exchanged buenos, he lit a small cigar. He was wearing well-worn modern cowboy clothes that must have been bought in the boys' department of a Western clothing store. He could not have weighed more than ninety pounds, and his hands and feet were very small.

"I was in New York once," he said, "with a Wild West show. That was a long time ago, before I was in the war."

"World War II?"

"The big war. With General MacArthur."

"Did you like being in the Wild West show?"

"I liked it best at nighttimes." He winked a bloodshot eye. "At nighttimes I could get in bed with the girls."

"Were you a stunt rider?"

He nodded. His aquiline nose was like an arrowhead driven out of the stretched brown skin of his face.

Across the way, tourists drifted along the sidewalk in front of the Palace of the Governors where Pueblos and Navajos were peddling their wares on spread blankets. In whispered conferences with prospective buyers the Indians offered discount deals.

At the sound of loud laughter, the Tewa turned and squinted toward a cream-colored hotel that sprawled across an adjoining square block. For twenty-four hours a day the place swarmed with conventioneers, companies of movie actors, and groups of elderly tourists arriving and departing by busloads. Several actors were coming out to board a station wagon parked beside the plaza. They were going north to one of the canyons where they were filming a Western movie. The chief actor who was playing the role of an Indian in the movie was of Italian descent. When he smiled, which he did often, he showed his perfect white artificial teeth that looked even more artificial against his dark skin. He was surrounded by bit players and girls, all talking very loudly.

The Tewa squinted at them until the station wagon rolled out of sight up the old Santa Fe Trail. "Young people don't have enough to do these days," he said. "They can't spend all time in bed with each other." He forced a bawdy grimace, exposing gaps between his stained teeth. "So they make up games to play."

"You said you were in the big war with General MacArthur. Did you go to the Philippines?"

"In the Philippines. And everywhere else in the Pacific Ocean."

"I was in the war," I said. "The Army liked to make scouts out of Indians and send them on dangerous missions. Did they make you a scout?"

He did not reply because he was absorbed in watching four young white men in yellow robes who had just entered the plaza. Their heads were shaven naked. They resembled middle-class college athletes of a few years ago who shaved their heads at the beginnings of football seasons. One of them began winding a length of yellow cloth into a turban around his bare head. Another propped a very large blown-up portrait photograph of an Oriental Indian in the center of the plaza bandstand, and then they began chanting and making a sort of music with sitars and other Oriental instruments. They called themselves the Hare Krishnas.

The Tewa was vastly amused. He uttered a sharp little yip and rubbed his small booted feet together.

"I was a scout," he said. "I was wounded twice in the Pacific. The second time they thought I would lose my leg, but I did not." He relit the end of his shortened cigar and faced the limestone memorial shaft in the center of the plaza.

The legend on it read:

TO THE HEROES
WHO HAVE FALLEN
IN VARIOUS BATTLES
WITH SAVAGE INDIANS
IN THE TERRITORY
OF NEW MEXICO.

The Tewa had probably seen it so many times he did not even know it was there anymore.

A police car pulled up in the street near the bandstand, and two policemen strolled over to query the Hare Krishnas. Because they were selling pamphlets they had to have a license. They had no license. The policemen waved two of the yellow-robed young men into the squad car and they drove away. The other pair carried on with the chanting.

"We were here in this pueblo country a long time before any other people," the Tewa said. "Now people come here from everywhere, from all over the world."

"They probably came from California," I said. "The ones in the yellow robes, I mean."

"Yes, but it is possible they have been all the way around the world more than once. Young people don't have enough to do these days, so they keep going around and around the world."

Because he used an occasional Spanish word in his conversation, I asked if he could speak Spanish. He rattled off something very fast. It sounded like Spanish.

"I'm sorry I don't speak Spanish very well," I said. "I know only a few words. You probably know Tewa, too."

"Tewas speak Taroan." He made a few sounds, but I could hear no words in them.

"I'm sorry. I don't understand."

"Are you deaf?" he shouted. He let out a loud Tewa yip like a war cry in a Western movie, and then he repeated the sounds he had made.

"No, I don't understand what you said. I don't know Taroan."

"I wasn't speaking Taroan." His eyes lit up triumphantly. "I was speaking Australian. I learned it when I was in the war with General MacArthur. Don't you know Australian?"

"It didn't sound like Australian to me."

"You lazy white people. If you had to be smart to live, like the Tewas, you would learn the languages of the people in the places where you go."

The police car brought back the Krishnas in their yellow robes. Now they had a permit, and they began selling pamphlets. They also resumed chanting and making noises with their Oriental instruments. "Holly looba, holly Krishna," they chanted repeatedly.

The Tewa listened politely until the sounds finally died away. "Young people don't have enough to do in these times," he said. "They have to make up games to play."

"You said you were a trick rider in a Wild West show. Did you ever compete in rodeos?"

"Every year when I was younger I went to the rodeos and rode for the prizes. After my leg got shot up in the war I could not go anymore."

"You don't even go to watch?"

"No."

"Don't you miss all the excitement?"

"I miss the nighttimes at the rodeos." He sat up straight, remembering, feeling good from the whiskey he'd had earlier that morning, and then he let out that shrill Tewa yip again. "I liked the rodeos best at nighttimes. Then I could get into bed with the girls."

CHAPTER EIGHT

The Great Depression of the 1930s

BY THE TIME I GRADUATED FROM Arkansas State Teachers College in 1931, I had applied to various universities where library science was taught and had narrowed my choices down to two. In the world outside of the sheltered college campus, the greatest economic depression of our times waited for us like a treacherous quagmire. We were aware that jobs were hard to find, and I knew that I must earn my way through graduate school. Should I go to the University of Illinois in the small town of Urbana, or George Washington University in Washington, D.C.? I took this quandary to my college mentor, Dean McBrien. Go to the nation's capital, he advised immediately. A year in Washington would be an education in itself. The capital was a prosperous city; part-time employment should be easy to find. Fifteen years later, I finally reached the University of Illinois as a professional librarian, but I followed McBrien's advice and went first to Washington. He was right about the city being an education in itself and about its relative prosperity, but he was wrong about good jobs being easy to find.

When I arrived there, even the nation's capital was affected by the Great Depression that was engulfing the world. From all across the country, college graduates by the hundreds, along with aging veterans of World War I, were pouring into Washington seeking employment or military bonuses. I found a place to sleep in a basement room with seven other college graduates, our cots pushed together in a solid line. One man boasted a Ph.D., and appropriately he had the best job of the lot of us. He drove a taxicab.

George Washington University's library school no longer exists, but in the 1930s its small faculty was supplemented by dozens of visiting professional librarians from government agencies and other institutions in the capital. By working as a part-time elevator operator, janitor, tire repairman, and filling station jockey, I managed to pay for one or two night courses each semester in the university. After I went to work nights for Willard Marriott, I had to switch to day classes, and eventually I dropped out.

Marriott opened the first drive-in barbecue stands in Washington, one near the baseball park where the old Senators team played, the other on the edge of the District of Columbia near Chevy Chase, Maryland. From their small beginnings grew the billion-dollar Marriott empire. He called them Hot Shoppes and developed a system for serving customers at no expense to himself. The pretty girls he employed took orders from customers in their automobiles, then rushed into the Hot Shoppe, purchased the sandwiches and drinks, and delivered them on a tray attached to the car doors. Tips were their only income, and if the girls were busy with several customers and one drove off without paying, the girls were out of pocket for whatever they had paid for the food and drinks.

To prevent such thefts and to remove trays from cars ready to leave, as well as to stop quarrels over territorial rights among the girls, Marriott employed a male known as a curbmaster. That was the job that I endured for several months. The salary was small, but after midnight the girls departed and a curbmaster could pick up a few tips serving trays to night owls. During the midwinter months, however, business was so slow that almost all of us were laid off until spring.

That winter was the very depth of the Great Depression, the last weeks of President Hoover and the first days of President Roosevelt who brought his New Deal to Washington and changed it from a somnolent Southern town into an exciting and glittering city.

For a few weeks after leaving the Hot Shoppes, I worked as a tire repairman for the Firestone Tire and Rubber company, but on the payday before Roosevelt's inauguration, the company announced that checks would be delayed because of a shortage of funds. On the day of the inaugural parade, the manager closed the station and we all walked down to Pennsylvania Avenue to watch the passing sights. All of us wondered if the new president could arrange to get our paychecks issued. If a large corporation like

Firestone could not pay its bills, we were very dubious about our future.

Soon after Roosevelt took over the White House, he created the Civilian Conservation Corps, which was meant to provide employment for thousands of young men who could not find work. The Three C's, as the corps was called, engaged in reforestation, fighting forest fires, and related activities. Hundreds of camps were established, mostly in the Southern states, and when I learned that Arkansas would be heavily engaged, nostalgia and a desire for something more permanent brought me back home for a time.

Within a few days I was inducted into the corps and assigned to a camp near Hot Springs. The life in the woods that I had looked forward to, however, soon came to an end. On my application paper, I had checked the affirmative box after the question: *Can you type?* As male typists were in short supply in the CCC, I was quickly transferred back to Little Rock headquarters.

There I became a secretary of sorts for a colonel who was in charge of all the camps in Arkansas. In order to bring the CCC into hasty but orderly organization, its founders used military officers, mostly reservists. Because a large segment of the American public feared that the corps was a scheme to enlarge the Army, the officers usually wore civilian clothing. The men, however, were issued old uniforms that had been in storage since World War I, and they wore them while working. I wore the woolen khaki trousers most of the time, but because the shirts were too warm for office work, I used my own.

The hundred or so men in the headquarters company were housed in an old warehouse adjoining a railroad track in east Little Rock. Most of them either serviced or drove the trucks that hauled supplies to camps all over the state; only four or five men were assigned to the headquarters office in the YMCA building on Broadway.

Overlord of the old warehouse was a retired Army sergeant who had been called back to duty, a crusty but forgiving man who roused us out of our bunks every morning at six by turning on the lights and blowing a shrill whistle. As soon as we were dressed we were hustled out upon the grounds where we stood formation while he called the roll. For some reason he dubbed us the Algerian Army, and almost every morning he expressed a wish that he could drill us and shape us into respectable doughfeet. Drilling, however, was forbidden in the CCC. Some early PR person in Washington decided that we should be called "Peaveys" after the hooked hand lever used by loggers, but I do not recall the sergeant or anyone else using that term to address us.

Because Little Rock was my hometown, with friends and relatives in abundance, I seldom spent evenings before bedtime in the old warehouse. On the occasions that I did, I enjoyed listening to the adventures of the truck drivers. One of the drivers was Irish-born, and he almost convinced me that he frequently encountered leprechauns on the road to Devil's Den, a camp in the Ozarks. "A tiny little fellow he was, a-standin' in the road, daring me to climb out of me truck and follow him to his buried gold. Had I done so, I daresay y'd never seen me again."

My duties in the headquarters were fairly light except on Mondays, the day when weekly reports were due from every camp. I assembled them in alphabetical order for the colonel to examine and respond to, and then he would pass them back to me to extract the names and home addresses of each recruit absent without leave. The only punishment for deserting a camp was a form letter addressed to the recruit's parents, notifying them that their son's absence without leave had extended to a dishonorable discharge.

A large number of young men from the northern Plains, the Dakotas mostly, had been brought down to the Ozarks camps, which were usually set up in a hollow or clearing with a green wall of trees around them. Many of these recruits went absent without leave, and when they were picked up a day or so later trying to hitchhike home, they usually gave their reason for deserting as "sick of looking at trees" or "fear of trees." Growing up on the Great Plains, they had grown accustomed to vast treeless distances.

When I typed the dozens of reported absences on Mondays, I began noting that most of the camp commanders gave "fear of trees" as the reason for desertion. Therefore, I typed that phrase on the proper line. One day the colonel called me to his desk and pointed to a sheaf of discharges he had signed. "I don't like this reason we give for going over the hill," he said. "'Fear of trees' is not dignified. I want you to find me a dignified word."

So I walked over to my favorite place in town, the Little Rock Public Library, and dug into the dictionaries. I found "arboloco" right away, but going mad from trees did not seem quite dignified to me. After some thought, I coined "arbophobia." The colonel accepted it with thanks, and from that day we used the big dignified word on all our discharge letters.

During the weeks that I had worked in Washington, I took every Civil Service examination that I felt qualified for. One evening when I returned to quarters in the warehouse, an official-looking letter was waiting for me. A minor library position was open in the Food and Drug Administration, then a division of the Department of Agriculture.

After reporting for duty at the Food and Drug Administration library, I reentered night classes at George Washington University. While I was completing work for a library degree, I was fortunate enough to persuade Sally Stroud to marry me. We had known each other only casually during college days, but after she came to Washington to work for the New Deal we met again and became more than friends. Sally was from northeast Arkansas, and she charmed me with her creamy Delta accent. We also had similar backgrounds, her mother having died when Sally was a child, leaving her a half-orphan like me. She loved books, wrote poetry, told funny stories, and had lots of sex appeal.

Sally fascinated me with her tales of growing up on the Wilson Plantation, which was probably the last realm ruled by one man in the entire Mississippi Valley. The Byzantine emperor of this vast agricultural land was a benevolent despot named Robert E. Lee Wilson. He was sole owner of the plantation and everything except the post office in the town of Wilson, Arkansas.

After Sally graduated from Wilson High School with the highest honors in the class, she realized that her father could not afford to send her to college and so she applied to a beautician school in Memphis and was accepted. The day before she was to leave for Memphis, Robert E. Lee Wilson, who kept track of every soul in his

Sally and Dee Brown (fourth and fifth from left) with friends at Romany Marie's in Greenwich Village, late 1930s

domain, discovered what she was planning to do. He rode his horse up to her front porch and told her he had changed her plans. Instead of going to Memphis the next morning, she boarded a train bound for the Arkansas State Teachers College at Conway, armed with a scholarship provided by the Byzantine emperor. Whatever his faults may have been, I have always had a soft spot in my heart for R.E.L. Wilson. If he had not sent Sally to college, we would never have met.

Another of her amusing stories concerned the benevolent despot's method of stopping the Frisco passenger train at the Wilson station. For business reasons, he had to make semiweekly trips to Memphis, but automobile travel was slow and uncertain over the unpaved highways of that time. The Frisco Railroad, however, consistently refused to provide service to passengers from the town of Wilson on the grounds that so few people ever boarded.

The Frisco, however, was not the only railroad that served the town. R.E.L. Wilson owned a short line whose track crossed the Frisco's in order to reach the plantation's sawmill and cotton gin. After several polite requests to the Frisco to make signaled stops long enough for him to board and receiving only negative replies, Mr. Wilson at certain times on certain days began ordering his little freight train to stop in the act of crossing the Frisco track. And so, twice each week, while the Frisco locomotive engineer waited impatiently for the track to clear, R.E.L. Wilson would climb aboard the parlor car at the rear of the passenger train and seat himself like the potentate he was for a comfortable ride into Memphis.

Those were exhilarating times in Washington during the early 1930s. Roosevelt surrounded himself with several brilliant men and women of good intentions, as well as a few eccentrics who made life interesting. During this same period, the voters out in the states were electing congressmen several notches above the old-line politicians who had let the country slide into economic stagnation and despair. Most of these lively newcomers to the federal government made themselves available in frequent meetings large and small, so that everyone in Washington had a sense of participation in the various New Deal programs that we seriously believed were keeping the nation from collapsing.

Brown (middle) with WPA writers Jack Conroy (left) and Nick Ray, Washington, D.C., 1938

One enterprise that especially appealed to me was the Federal Writers Project. If I had not been fortunate enough to receive promotions and transfers into better jobs within the Department of Agriculture Library system, I would have made an earnest effort to join the Writers Project, which eventually created a considerable body of badly needed American source materials, including those wonderful WPA guidebooks to the states. After more than half a century, these books are so esteemed that most of them are kept continually in print.

Several friends worked in the Writers Project, so I was often invited to their Sunday gatherings and occasional weekend jaunts and hikes into the Blue Ridge Mountains. Best remembered are Ben Botkin, the folklorist; Jack Conroy, the proletarian author and editor; Jerry Mangione, who eventually wrote the project's history; John Cheever, before he became famous; and Vardis Fisher, who occasionally came in from Idaho.

I admired these people, and it was largely through knowing them that I began submitting manuscripts to the numerous "little magazines" that were springing up to set the world to right. A short story I wrote that was based upon experiences at the drive-in barbecue was published in one of them and subsequently noticed by a New York literary agent, Mavis McIntosh. An inquiry from her as to whether I might have a novel in progress inspired me to start one immediately.

I decided to try a satire on the burgeoning bureaucracy of New Deal Washington. Compared to our present governmental bureaucracy—which is so pervasive that it would be impossible to satirize—the New Deal's was a fairly light-hearted state of confusion rather than total bedlam. The phenomenon of bumbledom was new to almost everybody, and I thought it had its amusing aspects. And so in a novel I pummeled the government in a broad way. During the months that followed, my novel and World War II moved simultaneously into unforeseen climaxes.

CHAPTER NINE

The Greatest Sheep Dog in the World

JUST AS I WAS BEGINNING TO DEVISE A PLOT and develop the characters for my untitled satirical novel of New Deal Washington, I received a promotion and was transferred to the Beltsville Research Center. My assignment was to build a library from scratch to serve several different research stations and laboratories spread across a wide expanse of Maryland countryside. This new responsibility, of course, slowed down my literary endeavors.

The four years that I worked in the Beltsville library were the most interesting of the various periods I spent in federal agencies. Scientists in the biological, chemical, and medicinal fields were on the verge of discoveries that would bring immense changes not only to American agriculture but in many other areas of American life. A sense of exciting discovery was evident among many of the people I worked with, and this acted as a spur for us to furnish them with the best informational service that we could.

Because they expected to be kept up to date in their various endeavors, we circulated a large number of current scientific journals and newly published books. To keep these publications moving about the research center, we first tried a motorcycle. In order to keep in touch with the scientists that I was serving, I frequently joined our motorcycle driver in his reckless deliveries to the scattered laboratory buildings. Hunkered down in the sidecar with heaps of books and journals piled around and on me, I more than once thought as we sped along, *What a hell of a way to run a library.* But I met several fascinating researchers, some of whom were making their marks in the world of scientific agriculture.

There were also frequent visitors from everywhere around the world, as well as magazine writers and photographers in search of stories. The most famous columnist who came occasionally was

Eleanor Roosevelt, looking for interesting things at Beltsville to put into her syndicated column, "My Day." Mrs. Roosevelt did not always get the correct spin on the research that was revealed to her, and the Beltsville administrators who were always eager for good publicity that might bring additional appropriations from Congress were sometimes uneasy about her comments.

For a year or so, one research project was kept off limits to Mrs. Roosevelt and to almost everyone else. I would probably have known very little about the Sheep Dog Project had I not taken a sidecar journey over there one day and won the confidence of Dr. Morton, the chief, and his animal psychologist, Dr. Katz.

A few weeks later, I learned about the Turkish sheep dogs that came very near creating an international incident in the critical days just before our entry into World War II. My first awareness of these Turkish dogs came one morning when Dr. Morton swept suddenly into my office in the Beltsville library. Morton's specialty had been sheep breeding, but he had been drafted into the Dog Project by the Secretary of Agriculture, Henry A. Wallace. Secretary Wallace was an extraordinary man, as were most of the New Dealers. He had a large role in the development of hybrid corn, a triumph of genetics, and after he became Roosevelt's Secretary of Agriculture he kept up his interest in the transmission of genetic traits.

Wallace liked dogs, believed them to be unusually intelligent animals, and decided to establish a project at Beltsville in which their intelligence traits could be studied through many succeeding generations. He knew that Congress would never appropriate money for so pure a scientific project as this; therefore he disguised it as research to determine what breed of dog was the most efficient sheep dog. In those days manmade fibers were in their infancy, and almost every state in the Union had numerous sheep raisers who were hard at work producing honest wool. They were all interested in good sheep dogs. Wallace named this research program the Sheep Dog Project, and as further camouflage he placed the chief sheep husbandman, Dr. Morton, in charge of it.

The morning that Morton entered the Beltsville library, his face was flushed, he was short of breath, and obviously in desperate need of some specific piece of information. When people appear in a library in such condition, librarians usually wince inwardly. Over-eager seekers of information tend to follow one about, peering over one's shoulder as the search goes on. Librarians have precious few trade secrets, and some of these may inadvertently be revealed to a client who is desperate and in a hurry.

"I'm looking for a parasitic worm," Morton explained. "Cestode, probably. I must identify it right away."

The problem seemed simple until he added: "Not known in this country. Probably Middle Eastern. Turkey." He was still breathing hard. "Very dangerous, they say. When transmitted to humans."

By one of those strokes of luck that keep reference librarians from losing their jobs, I found what Morton was looking for in a thick old volume that had been published early in the century. He peered at a drawing of a cobra-shaped worm and read the legend beneath it. "I was afraid of that," he said, shaking his head. "The Turks won't like it if we have to destroy one of their dogs."

I knew about the Scotch Border collies and the Hungarian pulis over at the Dog Project, but Turkish dogs were something new. "Whose dogs? Turks, you said?" I asked, but Morton was already in motion, his fingers thrust into the book to hold the proper page, as he disappeared through the entranceway.

It was a fine sunny day, and as soon as the noon break came, I collected my sack lunch and bottle of milk from the biological chemist's refrigerator down the hall and set out for the Dog Project on the adjoining rise. In those days Beltsville was rolling meadows and trees, and if we didn't play an inning of softball during the lunch hour we usually walked somewhere to see what was happening in other areas of the research center.

With appropriations received from Congress, Secretary Wallace had already built two rows of kennels, with exercise yards adjoining, and the Scotch Border collies and Hungarian pulis were well into their second and third generations. As I walked past I could see that all pens were occupied, and I wondered where space could be found for another breed of dogs. At one end of the kennels was a small office building. The first door bore a sign: JUNIOR DOG KENNELMAN AND UNDER DOG KENNELMAN. (These are actual job nomenclature titles and can be found in the Civil Service

Getting a man out at first, Beltsville Research Center, Maryland, 1940

Commission's list of government positions for the 1930s, but would be considered sexist today.)

The office of the junior dog kennelman and under dog kennelman was empty. The kennelmen were probably over in the sheep pasture testing some of the dogs. The next door was labeled DR. KATZ. He was in and was just opening up his lunch. On the wall behind him was a large handmade poster with dozens of names of dogs laid out in genealogical charts.

At that time Dr. Katz had not yet changed his name, but a few months later he did. The Dog Project had a daily round of visitors from all over the country, some of them being accompanied by Secretary Wallace. Several times each day whoever might be conducting the visitors would gleefully say to them: "This is Dr. Katz, the dogs' psychologist." After suffering the inevitable repeated jokes about Katz and dogs until he could no longer endure their monotony, Katz had his name legally changed.

He was an energetic, enthusiastic, very jolly young man who knew every one of the dogs in his care as thoroughly as a mother knows the individualities of her children. He was especially fond of the Hungarian pulis, and could tell very amusing stories about their cleverness. "They are too intelligent, really," he would say. "Like most sensitive personalities they have days of moodiness. At such times they tend to neglect their duties and permit the sheep to stray. Hungarian pulis just don't make good bureaucrats. They get bored watching dumb sheep all day. I think they would like to do something creative if we would only let them. I'm working on it."

I told him about Dr. Morton and the parasitic worm. "What's all this about Turkish dogs?" I asked.

"You haven't heard about the Turkish sheep dogs?" he asked. "No, I suppose not. We just learned about them yesterday. Secretary Wallace handled the details himself, and he's been too busy to keep us informed."

Katz proceeded to fill in the background, referring occasionally to a heap of letters and cablegrams that had been sent out from Washington. As he did not seem to mind, I scanned a few of them while he talked. Some weeks before, Wallace had attended a formal White House dinner where he was seated next to the Turkish ambassador. During the dinner he happened to mention the Dog Project, explaining that one of its objectives was to determine what breed made the best sheep dog.

"But that has already been determined," declared the Turk. "The best sheep dog is our Turkish sheep dog."

Wallace confessed his ignorance. "I was not aware of the Turkish breed," he said.

"Perhaps that is because we consider them to be so valuable that we do not export them from Turkey," the ambassador replied. "However, in the interest of science which is international, perhaps I can arrange for a male and a female to be obtained for your project."

"That would be splendid," said Wallace politely, and then soon afterward forgot all about the conversation. During the next few weeks he was away from Washington much of the time, making speeches in the agricultural states in support of Roosevelt's embattled farm programs. He was not available, therefore, the day a mysterious cablegram was received in one of the offices of the State Department:

HOLDING TWO TURKISH SHEEP DOGS ISTANBUL. REQUIRE CUS-
TODIAN BEFORE SHIPMENT CAN BE AUTHORIZED UNITED
STATES.

The message was signed by a Turkish port official, but the State Department people evidently believed it to be some kind of code. They bucked it around, hoping it would reach an official who might understand it, until at last somebody decided to telephone the Turkish embassy for a clarification.

After some delay, the ambassador himself explained the situation. He had personally arranged for the gift of a male and a bitch to be sent from Turkey to the Department of Agriculture's Sheep Dog Project. Animals as rare and valuable as Turkish sheep dogs, he insisted, would require a full-time attendant for so long a sea voyage. Perhaps an American naval vessel might be cruising somewhere in the vicinity of Istanbul?

No, he was informed politely, none of the U.S. Navy's ships was available at the time, and even if one had been, the State Department could scarcely order an admiral to take a pair of dogs under his command. The problem was one for the Turkish government and the Department of Agriculture's Sheep Dog Project to resolve between them. At this juncture the State Department washed its hands of the affair by sending the cablegram over to Secretary Wallace's office for action. Wallace was not there, of course, and as none of his assistants knew anything at all about the dogs, the message was put in a suspense file to await his return.

About a week later another cablegram arrived in Washington from Istanbul:

> TURKISH SHEEP DOGS DEPARTED THIS DATE IN CUSTODY TWO
> SAILORS ABOARD SS OCHRIDA. BOTH IN GOOD HEALTH.

When Wallace read this one during a short stopover in Washington between speeches, he apparently made no comment to anyone in his office, nor did he find time to notify the Sheep Dog Project about the forthcoming arrivals. He may have called the Turkish ambassador to thank him and perhaps comment on the health of the dogs and/or sailors, but there was no record of it.

During succeeding weeks, cables arrived at Wallace's office from Italy, North Africa, and Spain—wherever the steamship *Ochrida* happened to put into port—each one giving brief descriptions of the sheep dogs' dispositions, their appetites, weight, and coat conditions. Then finally a telegram came from New York announcing their arrival on American soil, their passage through customs, and the approximate time they would reach the Beltsville Research Center. A few hours later the Dog Project heard for the first time of the Turkish sheep dogs. Dr. Morton immediately notified the official station veterinarian, and the two men met the express train that brought the Turkish dogs into the quiet Maryland railroad stop.

Tests on the male showed that he was in perfect health, as the cables had claimed, but the bitch was afflicted with that rare and dangerous cestode which Morton later identified in the library. This was as much as Dr. Katz could tell me, and he was not surprised by my informing him that Dr. Morton had left the library in a distraught condition, clutching the book on parasites in his hand.

Next day I happened to meet Morton in the parking lot. "How is the Turkish bitch doing?" I asked.

"Not good, not good," he replied.

"Can't the veterinarian rid her of that parasite?"

He shook his head. "Not positively without risking her life. But we're calling in a research man from a private laboratory—he's supposed to have something new. You know, we simply must admit that bitch to our Sheep Dog Project or we're going to cause international trouble. The Turkish ambassador is pressing us for news photographs and a big publicity release about the universality of science and the part Turkey has played in advancing knowledge by presenting us with these dogs. The Turks have gone to a lot of trouble and expense to get the dogs to us, and if we destroy the bitch they'll think we're not decent people." He sighed and shook his head again sadly. "With that war heating up again in Europe," he added, "everybody knows we're bound to get involved, and we'll need all the friends we can find around the world. We can't afford to anger the Turks."

"What does Secretary Wallace think about the problem?"

"He doesn't know about it. He's out in the Nebraska farm country mending political fences. I talked with his wife last night, and she says I'd better not let the veterinarian destroy that dog before Henry comes back to Washington."

I could see that Morton was becoming distraught again. He looked as if he hadn't slept for two days.

"Perhaps you can keep the bitch in quarantine indefinitely," I suggested.

"That would be complicated," he replied solemnly. "She's pregnant."

Fortunately, the Dog Project's last hope, the research scientist from out of town, saved the situation. He had a new and secret chemical formula for completely eliminating internal parasites, and after a three-way telephone conversation with Secretary Wallace on the line from Nebraska, it was decided to risk the formula on the Turkish bitch. After a few days, results were pronounced satisfactory, and the veterinarian admitted both animals to the Sheep Dog Project. It was a gala occasion, with newspaper photographers and the Turkish ambassador present for the formalities.

Next morning I went over to the kennels to have my first look at the Turkish sheep dogs. I had to wait several minutes in a line of curious people outside the exercise yard. The Turks were housed in the largest of the kennels. A length of heavyweight wire fencing had been hastily fastened over the original thin wire. But even this added safeguard did not forestall a sudden jab of awe that seemed to affect each spectator when he or she first saw the dogs. They were gigantic, about the size of young colts. Their coats were dull gray and they had large bushy tails; their heads were wolflike and their feet were great heavy pads as large as dinner plates.

After several days, the commotion over the arrival of the Turkish sheep dogs gradually died down, but it was revived again when the bitch gave birth to twelve puppies. It was not so much the number of the litter but rather the size of each offspring that aroused comment. At the first opportunity, I went over to pay my compliments to the project's new arrivals. I found Dr. Katz staring moodily at the puppies in their sunny yard, an area which had been more than adequate for the collies and pulis but was far too small for these twelve young giants, padding about on feet already as large as saucers.

"They're bigger than most full-grown dogs," I said.

"And no discipline," Katz commented. "Absolutely no discipline." The young Turks were squirming about like monstrous worms, mouths open until they touched a neighboring ear or flesh, whereupon the jaws would clamp shut savagely. "This litter is very late establishing a chain of dominance—pecking order, you know. Until a chain is established, their anarchistic tendencies will keep the veterinarian busy patching up wounds."

The dogs paused momentarily as if they had overheard, staring at us in an unusually hostile manner. Katz shouted a jolly profanity at them, but there was a troubled look in his eyes.

"What did you do with the young pulis you had in here?" I asked.

"That's another problem," Katz said. "We had to move them over to the sheep barn. These Turks are crowding us out."

One might have thought that Katz and Morton, like proper government bureaucrats, should have been happy to have their project grow so rapidly. Instead, each time I saw them, they had bitter complaints to make about the Turks. The overcrowding was making all the dogs and the men who worked with them very nervous and irritable.

Some weeks after the birth of the Turkish pups, Katz showed up in the library in search of all the data we could find on nutrient requirements for dogs. For an hour or more he scribbled into a notebook; then he came into my inner office to light up his pipe. "We're in real trouble," he said. "The Turks' food consumption is rising exponentially. The twelve pups are eating more than all the other dogs combined. By the end of this month we'll be completely out of rations."

"Can't Secretary Wallace set up an emergency fund for you?" I asked.

"No. There's a temporary freeze on because of the military crisis. Dr. Morton persuaded the director of the center to shift some sheep funds to carry us another month, and then he sent a memo to the secretary's office suggesting that the Turks be sold as government surplus in order to save the rest of the Dog Project. But the administrative people are afraid that would offend the Turkish government." He shook his head gloomily.

"What're you going to do now?" I asked.

He shrugged. "I'd hoped we might be able to borrow foodstuffs from other Beltsville projects, but it won't work out. All we can do is fend off starvation. Dr. Morton scrounged some scraps from the Meats Division, but that just whetted the Turks' appetites." He knocked out his pipe and squinted through my office door at the bookstacks. "I envy you librarians. You don't have to feed your damned books, and they stay put when you want them to." He got up and walked away, his shoulders hunched forward, hands clasped behind his back.

Not long afterward I chanced to meet one of the kennelmen, who told me that an epidemic of dysentery had broken out in the Border collie kennels. "Poor nutrition and too much crowding," he explained glumly. "Dr. Katz is working eighteen hours a day trying to keep his record of experiments from being washed out. The dysentery wouldn't have been so bad if it had hit the Turk pups. They seem to thrive on dysentery germs."

The Turks not only survived but grew larger day by day, demanding more and more food. In the midst of this crisis, we suddenly entered World War II. Secretary Wallace was immediately drawn into the emergency food programs vital to the war effort, and neither he nor anyone else in Washington had time to consider the plight of the Sheep Dog Project. A brief note from the secretary's office informed Dr. Morton that operation of the Sheep Dog Project would thenceforth be the joint responsibility of the Beltsville Research Center's director and himself.

Morton wasted no time in arranging a meeting with the director. Out of stark necessity they quickly decided to declare the Turkish sheep dogs government surplus and hold a discreet public sale. Surely in the wake of Pearl Harbor, they hoped, neither the press nor the Turkish embassy would take notice of their action.

A few mimeographed announcements of the sale were run off and mailed out to a select list of sheepmen in nearby Maryland and Virginia. All of us who knew about this waited hopefully the morning of the advertised sale and were quite relieved when the first sheepmen began arriving on the main parking lot. Morton and Katz escorted them in small groups to the kennels. Out of curiosity I joined one of the groups—five men from western Maryland—and went along to see how the bidding was going. When we reached the Turks' kennel, the sheepmen stared with dismay at the monsters behind the heavy wire. It was obvious from their comments that the last thing they were willing to do was to allow one of those Turkish dogs within ten miles of their herds. Not one offered to bid, and from Dr. Katz I learned that none of the other sheepmen had made an offer either.

Late that afternoon I was in the director's office. I had received my draft notice from Selective Service, and he wanted my recommendations for a possible replacement for me from among the librarians in the Department of Agriculture. While we were going over the names, Dr. Morton barged in, angry and dejected. "Not a single bid on the Turks," he said. "*Nobody* wants them."

The director was equally disappointed.

"Why don't you make up a press release?" I suggested.

"You know we can't do that!" Morton shouted. "The Turkish

Dee and Sally Brown with Ivan, one of the greatest sheep dogs in the world, 1940

government would surely see it and take offense." He glared at me. "You're getting out of it the easy way by going into the Army. Here we are stuck with fourteen dogs eating up our last rations, and you're running off to the Army."

I couldn't see the logic of this, but I said soothingly, "Well, anyway, you've kept Turkey neutral in the war. I won't have to fight Turkish soldiers."

The next week I went into the Army, and it was some months later before I returned to Washington on a brief furlough. Occasionally, through the rigors of basic training, I'd given thought to the dilemma of the Turkish sheep dogs, and one of the first telephone calls I made after I returned home was to the Dog Project.

An unfamiliar voice answered. "K-Nine Corps. Sergeant Breen here."

I asked to speak with either Katz or Morton.

"They are no longer here," the sergeant said. "Sir, this is a military dog operation now. K-Nine Corps."

The sergeant did volunteer the information that one of the kennelmen had been held over from the civilian project. I asked to speak with him.

When I heard the familiar voice of the Under Dog Kennelman, I identified myself and asked how everything was going.

"Nothing like the old days," he answered. "Strictly GI now. All German police dogs. We're training them for combat and guard duties."

"I've been wondering," I said, "whatever happened to the Turkish sheep dogs."

"Oh, them. Not long after you left, we received an unexpected bid from a man who lives in the Virgin Islands. He showed up one day and carried off all fourteen of the Turks in a big truck."

"What did he want with them?" I asked. "All fourteen?"

There was a momentary pause. "Hell, I guess nobody thought to ask him, we were so damned glad to be rid of them."

After I hung up the phone, I sat down and thought about fourteen full-sized Turkish sheep dogs roaming over the verdant beauty of the Virgin Islands. And even now, all these years afterward, when I hear of or read about the Virgin Islands, I don't visualize green hills or clean sandy beaches lapped by rolling waves under azure skies. Instead I think of fourteen mammoth Turkish sheep dogs and all their hungry offspring overpopulating that tropical paradise.

CHAPTER TEN

Soldiering with the Goon Squad

RUNNING PARALLEL WITH MY CONTINUAL SURVEILLANCE of the last days of the Sheep Dog Project were my writing efforts—particularly the satirical novel about Washington. By working late at nights I managed to bring it to completion, and to my surprise the literary agent, Mavis McIntosh, placed the manuscript rather quickly with a small publisher in Philadelphia—Macrae-Smith. My editor-to-be was Edward Shenton, who was also an artist and had done illustrations for some of Marjorie Kinnan Rawlings' books about Florida. Shenton evidently liked my satirical novel. He suggested only a few changes, and had it copyedited for the printer late in November 1941.

On Sunday, December 7, my wife Sally and I joined half a dozen friends for lunch on Pennsylvania Avenue, and then we all went up to Capitol Hill to film one of our outlandish 8-millimeter home movies, inventing a spy plot as we went along. After shooting short scenes around the Capitol steps, the Library of Congress, and Union Station, someone had the idea of staging a scene in front of the Gayety, a burlesque theater on Ninth Street. While we were doing this, a sudden flurry of excitement came from an adjoining shooting gallery, where all the firing had stopped. The radio was turned up, and we kept hearing the words "Pearl Harbor." In a matter of minutes we knew that the Japanese had attacked Hawaii, but the full impact of this did not penetrate our frivolous peacetime brains as we bumbled around excitedly. A member of the group suggested that we rush in our cars to the War Department Building—which in those pre-Pentagon days was on the north side of the Potomac. There, we thought, we would photograph our spy actors walking through the imposing front entrance.

Of course that was never accomplished, and we came very near

Brown at work on the ill-fated satiric novel, 1940

losing our little camera to an earnest military policeman who charged upon us before we could set up a scene. The Army in Washington certainly acted with dispatch on the afternoon of Pearl Harbor. After we drove past the Japanese Embassy, where white smoke was coiling from a high chimney (burning secret papers?) we headed for home in what was then the wooded countryside of Glen Echo Heights. As we passed the reservoir at the Maryland line we were surprised to see a company of soldiers preparing bivouacs for guard duty around the capital's water supply. None of us could have believed at that moment that this unfamiliar phenomenon would continue for four years of war, four years that would separate most of us forever.

On December 8, the day after Pearl Harbor, I received a telephone call from Edward Shenton of Macrae-Smith in Philadelphia, a hurried and brief statement that he was coming down to Washington the next day on government business and would like to meet me in the bar of the old Willard Hotel. At the agreed hour I met him, and after a few preliminary remarks about the shock of war that had come with such suddenness upon us, he told me that his company could not publish my book. In wartime, he explained, especially when the nation appeared to be so unprepared and disorganized, any criticism of the government, no matter how mild, would be considered unpatriotic.

"You must have some plan for a second novel," he added. "Perhaps something patriotic."

I had nothing particular in mind, but I told him that I did. Stung by the loss of my ill-starred contemporary novel, I resolved to retreat into the nineteenth century, where I have remained ever since. During my boyhood, Grandmother Cranford had told me stories about Davy Crockett who, she said, had hunted bears with her father along Duck River in Tennessee. I wanted to write Crockett's biography, but I sensed there would be no time for the research, so I made his life story into a historical novel. In three months I had the manuscript ready, and in about the same length of time Macrae-Smith published my first book, *Wave High the Banner*, a title that Sally picked out of an obscure poem by Shelley.

A few weeks later I was in the Army doing basic training in

Tennessee with the 80th Infantry Division. After completing training we left our barracks for maneuvers along the same Duck River where my great-grandfather hunted bears with Davy Crockett. During the maneuvers one of my feet was injured in a truck accident that put me on limited service with a new assignment. The battalion commander put a sergeant and me into a jeep to keep the situation maps up to date. With the onset of cold weather, we moved northward with another division to reenact the Civil War's Battle of Stones River in the same area where it had been fought eighty years or so before.

For this exercise, the jeep, the maps, the sergeant, and I were assigned to an intelligence company commanded by Major James Warner Bellah, who was as much an amateur as the rest of us. Because he spent considerable time examining the battle maps, we saw Major Bellah frequently and soon learned that he was a student of American Indian guerrilla warfare. Somewhat like the heroes of the movie scripts he later wrote for John Ford and John Wayne, Bellah took daring risks. He led us behind the "enemy" lines where most of us were captured and imprisoned in the opposing division's stockade. Some of the men disparaged Major Bellah's way of doing things, but I thought he had style.

Before we won or lost the Battle of Stones River, there was a very unexpected turn of events. Late one afternoon, with traces of sleet beginning to fall from a gray sky, the company commander ordered the sergeant and me to pack our personal gear and board a supply truck that was returning to our division's base at Camp Forrest.

The sergeant, whose name was Sanders, and I boarded the truck and rode through the wintry night. The lights of Camp Forrest looked unreal behind a screen of freezing fog; and when the truck stopped we were told to enter what appeared to be a mess hall. Instead of food, however, we encountered sheets of paper on the tables. With several dozen other enlisted men, we were soon involved in another of the Army's paper tests. We were not informed of its purpose before we began or after we finished filling in the forms, but we did enjoy the warmth of a night in a barracks before returning to the Cumberland Mountains to resume the mock battle.

One morning several days later, while I was attempting to dig a foxhole in very hard and rocky ground, I was interrupted by an unfamiliar jeep that swung in beside me. An unfamiliar corporal was driving, and beside him sat Sergeant Sanders.

"Get your field pack," Sanders said. "We've been ordered into base."

"What for?"

"Don't know," he replied.

It was the recent test we had taken that brought us back to Camp Forrest. As soon as we arrived, we were ordered to join a single file of men who were entering a small wooden building used as a dispensary. After an hour or so of dragging our packs, rifles, and muddy entrenching tools in a slow shuffle forward, Sanders and I reached the entrance. Only one man entered at a time, and we were unable to question any of those who had gone ahead of us because they all exited through a door on the other side and were herded into trucks which rumbled away as soon as they were filled.

About five minutes after Sanders disappeared inside, the door opened again and a sergeant asked for my name and serial number and then motioned me to enter. The light inside was dim in contrast to the bright outdoors, and I could barely see the shadowy form of a bulky captain stirring about in a chair behind a table. After a moment's delay he called out my name.

"Yes, sir," I responded.

He then read off the name of the university I attended and degree I had obtained. "Is that correct?"

"Yes, sir."

"I see by your MOS that you were a farmer in civilian life. You went to college to become a farmer?"

"I was never a farmer," I replied. "I worked for the Department of Agriculture as a librarian."

"You were misclassified," the captain said.

"I know, sir—I've been trying to find a military librarian assignment ever since I got into the Army."

He shook his head in a pitying way. "Would you like to go back to college?"

The question was so unexpected that I could not reply for

several moments. Then I stammered: "Would that be officers' candidate school, sir?"

"No, it is not OCS," he replied in a tone that indicated he was weary of answering the question. "It will be a regular college or university. Not as yet designated."

"Sir, what is the purpose of my going back to college?"

"I'll be goddamned if I know, soldier. My orders are to interview each of you men who passed the examination. You have one of two alternatives. If you wish to go to college, the Army will send you. If you don't wish to go, you will return to your outfit."

"I'll take college, sir."

The captain grunted. "That's what they all say. Wish I could go with you, but this is strictly for enlisted men. Out that door."

I found Sergeant Sanders waiting in the half-filled truck. "What do you make of it?" I asked him.

He grinned. "Sounds like a good deal. I sure hope to hell they send me back to the University of Chicago."

Sanders and I and about a hundred others from Camp Forrest were sent to Auburn, Alabama. As was customary during World War II, we traveled by train, being fortunate enough to be assigned to Pullman cars for the night ride down to Auburn.

We arrived there on a fine spring morning, expecting to be met by the usual drab Army trucks. Instead, a scholarly looking Special Services major, accompanied by two aging professors from Alabama Polytechnic University, was there to greet us as though we were all long-lost relatives returning home. In a rich Alabama accent, the major was extremely apologetic because there was no transportation for us. "The campus is only a few blocks away," he announced in a loud shrill voice that all of us could hear. "Will one of the sergeants take over for the march?"

A young sergeant wearing Ranger shoulder patches volunteered to lead us, and with rifles and heavy barracks bags slung over our shoulders we started out, the major and the two professors serving as point men. We marched right through the little town, halting occasionally to shift our heavy bags from one shoulder to the other. If any survivors of the Civil War were then alive in

Brown (right) with a friend at the end of basic training, Camp Forrest, Tennessee, 1942

Auburn, they must have thought we were the retreating Confederate Army.

News of our arrival spread rapidly, and before we were halfway to the campus, a line of slow-moving cars formed an escort alongside us. Most of them were filled with pretty girls who waved and smiled and occasionally attempted imitation wolf whistles. At one of our brief halts to shift barracks bags, a PFC asked the major politely why we couldn't ride in the cars with the girls.

"That wouldn't be seemly," the major replied. He pointed ahead. "Besides, there's the campus right yonder."

Green leaves of spring were already out on the street trees, and birds were singing. We marched along in dappled shade, inhaling the aroma of honeysuckle and admiring the pretty girls. After weeks of mountain maneuvers, monotonous male companionship, chow lines in cold rain, sleeping on muddy ground, digging foxholes, and straddling slit trenches, Auburn was a vision of Heaven.

We drew up on a Bermuda-grass lawn beside a brand-new red-brick dormitory, and at the Ranger sergeant's command we faced about and dropped our barracks bags at our feet. We were still wearing our winter uniforms and the hot sun brought out the sweat.

"There," said the scholarly major. "Not bad at all, was it? Let me introduce myself. I am Major Whaley, your commanding officer during your stay in Auburn. You are now assigned to a Specialized Training and Reassignment Unit, or STAR as we call it. The dormitory just behind you will be your new quarters. I have been asked to caution you to be especially careful of the furnishings in the rooms to which you will be assigned, as this building was completed only last year and was designed for young women. The young women students, I must say, graciously gave up the building to us as a part of their war effort. We are still awaiting instructions from Washington concerning your duties here at STAR, but in the meantime we shall carry on as though you were in combat training. All sergeants will fall out for a conference with me. Other ranks will form single file and move into the dormitory for room assignments."

The interior of the dormitory was so delightful after what we had endured the past several months that I don't believe a single one of us even looked outside until lunchtime. We spent the morning transferring our gear from barracks bags to dresser drawers and closets, lolling on the thick Beautyrest mattresses, and wandering in and out of the shiny bathrooms just to admire the indoor plumbing. At noon, the sergeants summoned us outside for a roll call, and then we filed over to a dining hall where a corps of white-uniformed waitresses, all of whom looked like goddesses, served us manna.

That afternoon the sergeants took us out for some simple drilling and a few jog trots around the Auburn football practice field. At four o'clock we were sent back to the girls' dormitory to shower and sack out on the Beautyrest mattresses.

For three or four days we went through this easy routine, and then additional groups of men began arriving from training camps all over the South. By the end of the week, a thousand new recruits for STAR were installed in the Auburn dormitories. To keep everybody busy, the harried major introduced prolonged reveille and retreat ceremonies. The young sergeant from the Rangers—his name was Sims—had attended a military school, and he quickly took over direction of the time-killing pomp-and-ceremony duties. He and the major rigged up a system of outdoor loudspeakers and secured recordings of all the bugle calls known throughout history. All day long, from five A.M. until ten P.M., we were controlled by electronic bugles blaring mess call, mail call, sick call, recall, boots and saddles, and dozens of others.

Then one morning after a lengthy reveille ceremony, Major Whaley's friendly Alabama voice informed us over the loudspeakers that the purpose of our being there had at last been made clear by the Army. "After breakfast and the usual mail and sick calls, each dormitory unit will fall in and march to the main assembly hall. It is very important that every man be present by nine o'clock, and if for any reason anyone will be delayed or absent, I must be personally informed."

As far as I know, every man of the STAR unit was present at the appointed time. So great was the mass curiosity as to our fates, I am sure that nothing short of a paralyzing ailment could have kept any one of us away.

We were let down badly, however, by the scholarly major. All the information he had for us was that he had received a box of sealed examination papers from Washington. We were to take another test, and we were to take it right then and there. A group of civilian professors moved out among us, distributing the examination forms, and for the next two hours they hovered along the walls watching us to make certain that no one cheated. It was the most difficult test I had ever been subjected to, being weighted heavily with advanced mathematical problems. At the end of the two hours, I was sure that I had flunked it.

Not only I but nine out of ten of the STAR soldiers failed that test, and we heard about it the next day from Major Whaley in a general assembly.

"Young soldiers," he began, "it is my duty to inform you that only ten percent of STAR passed the engineering test. Naturally we had hoped for a higher rate. I am going to read off the names of those who passed the test, and at the end of this assembly these lucky young soldiers will report to Dormitory Four. We understand that orders are being cut now in Washington for their transfer to a Midwestern university where they will be given intensive courses in engineering. As for the remainder of you fine young men, we extend our thanks to you for being here as a part of STAR, and our regrets that you did not pass the examination. Sometime within the next few days you will receive orders transferring you back to your original units."

Our response to this announcement was a chorus of sincere moans. Not one of us then knew whether or not he had passed the test, and after our dreamlike interlude in the dormitories of Auburn, the thought of returning to barracks and pup tents, to chow lines and slit trenches, was too much to endure. All we could do was lament, and we did so with such force that poor Major Whaley looked as if he were about to join in our keening plaint.

Sergeant Sanders, who had come down from Camp Forrest with me, was one of the lucky achievers. A day or so later he and his fellow engineers departed for a campus somewhere in Indiana. The rest of us waited for those dreadful orders that would transfer us from Heaven back to Hell. During the interim Major Whaley—who felt sorry for us—relaxed STAR's time-killing routines and let rotating groups of us have passes to go into the town of Auburn. We quickly discovered that the townspeople knew all about our sad fate, of how we had somehow fallen short. But instead of regarding us as failures, the good people of Auburn viewed us as noble knights whose wounds needed healing. The matrons organized musicales; the young ladies held dancing parties. The Methodists, Baptists, and even the Presbyterians vied with each other in planning picnics, softball contests, and swimming meets. Day after day we were kept in a constant whirl. A strange drowsiness seemed to possess us so that we would have forgotten World War II altogether had it not been for all those luscious young ladies who kept reminding us that it was their duty to do everything in their power to provide us with easement from the horrors of war.

It all ended one morning with a summons to a general assembly. Flanked by a dozen Auburn professors, Major Whaley greeted us with jubilant Southern courtesy: "There's been a complete change of plans, young soldiers. I am happy to inform you that you are now full-fledged members of the ASTP, Army Specialized Training Program, that is. Recognizing that you are all men of special abilities, the Army has instructed us to run you through a battery of tests to determine in which fields of effort your special gifts may be best applied."

The tests began that morning, First we took a test to determine what kind of tests we were best suited to take. During the next five days we must have taken forty tests—language tests, geography tests, mathematical tests, biology tests, form and sound tests. The only way we could bear up under the monotonous scratching of pencils and shuffling of papers was to turn our memories back to bivouacs in the rain, kitchen police duty, and slit trenches. Then we would square our shoulders determinedly and march back into the examination room for one more test.

By the fourth day we were segregated into special groups, and there was a great deal of transferring of living quarters. One of my roommates went off to join the Arabic language group in Dormitory Five. Another went next door to join the predental group. On the fifth day I was ordered to move up to the top floor of the girls' dormitory where I found twenty-four other mystified test takers. As not one of us knew what our group was supposed to be, we decided to gather in one room and draw up a list of our civilian occupations, hoping this would give us some clue as to what our ASTP specialty would be. About a third had come into the Army directly from colleges, and they were discounted. Four or five had been schoolteachers, one a college instructor. One had been the operator of a gasoline station, one a newspaper reporter, another a clerk from the New York garment district. One declared himself to be an Amateur Psychologist. Another, whom we were soon to refer to as "Our PFC of Independent Means," because he always seemed to have plenty of money, classified himself as an unpublished poet. There was even a professional "Boy from Brooklyn" among us; he apparently had spent most of his young life memorizing the works of Damon Runyan, from which he could recite endlessly in varying shades of dialect. I was the only librarian. It soon became evident that there was no pattern among us, no common thread to link us as specialists of any kind.

One of the three sergeants in our group was young Sergeant Sims, and because of his rapport with Major Whaley we insisted that he call upon the commander and find out what we were supposed to be. Sims returned just before retreat ceremonies. "The major isn't quite certain of our nomenclature," he drawled in his Tennessee accent. "He said we were a very special group and to just rest easy until we get our orders."

In the days immediately following, our friends in the other groups began departing for other universities around the country where they would be studying special subjects that supposedly would make them more useful to the Army. In a week or so we were the last of the "veterans," and new detachments of soldiers began arriving to begin new cycles of tests. Each day Sergeant Sims visited Major Whaley, and each day he returned with no news of our fate. Rumors arose out of nowhere. We had been chosen for secret work behind enemy lines; we were to be flown to Russia for a very important mission; because of a shortage of chaplains we were going to a chaplain's school at the University of Utah. We suspected that the imaginative Boy from Brooklyn planted some of them, but at one time or another we believed all of them.

Late one afternoon, Sergeant Sims appeared suddenly on the

upper floor hallway with a huge bulging manila envelope. "Here it is, fellows! Our travel orders!"

We bounded out of our rooms, surrounding him. "What is it," somebody shouted, "the chaplains' school?"

Sims grinned. "Philadelphia," he said. "University of Pennsylvania."

A wiry corporal named Sam Feldman yelled: "My hometown!"

"What are we supposed to do there?" somebody asked.

"We're going to become personnel psychologists," Sims replied. "Whatever that means."

We left Auburn early the next morning, twenty-five of us in our own private Pullman car, which bore the name of John Jay. One of our members who had been a history teacher declared that this was a good omen because John Jay had been a great traveler during the formative years of the American Republic. We accepted his judgment and settled down for a pleasant ride. As we passed through Georgia, one of our members, a sardonic tech-sergeant named Bill Gnann, bemoaned the fact that but for the stupidities of the Army he could have been enjoying the recent wasted weeks in his hometown of Savannah. When we reached North Carolina, PFC Tom Marlowe repeated the same remark and invited us to join him in a mass AWOL expedition to his hometown. If we had known what lay ahead of us, we probably would have begged him to lead us into the hills.

During the night as we rolled northward, I dreamed that I was Nikolai Lenin traveling with my revolutionary associates in a sealed train across enemy territory. In the dream I was troubled because I could not remember the purpose of the journey, and I awoke very much disturbed. Through the curtains of the old-fashioned Pullman berth, I saw three or four of my companions in one of the forward seats; they were wrapped in blankets and playing cards unenthusiastically. As it was cold in the John Jay, I took a blanket and joined them. None of them really wanted to play cards at that hour of the morning; they wanted to talk about the purpose of our journey.

"The way I figure," the Amateur Psychologist said, "the Army has drained off all the students, and the colleges are about to go bust. That's why they hatched up this ASTP, to save the colleges."

"No," the Historian disagreed, "I think it's deeper than that. Back in World War I, the British sent off all their brightest young men to die and they lost a whole generation of brains and leaders. That almost finished off the British. Maybe somebody high up in our government remembered that and devised ASTP as a means of keeping our bright young men out of combat."

"Good God," said the former clerk from the New York garment district, "you have a high opinion of yourself, don't you. What makes you think we're any better than those poor dogfaces we left back in the training camps?"

"We passed the tests, didn't we?"

"It proves only that we're just smart at passing tests. Nothing else."

Sergeant Sims shivered under his blanket. "I'd rather be back in the Rangers. At least I knew what I was doing there. What the hell is a personnel psychologist?"

"They fit people into their proper niches," the Amateur Psychologist replied. "It's not my field, but I'll take it before infantry intelligence any day."

About midmorning we rolled into the Philadelphia railroad station. The train crew helped us unload our swollen barracks bags and we made them into a small mountain on the platform. Sergeant Sims went off with his big manila envelope to see if he could find somebody from the University of Pennsylvania. He was gone a long time, and when he returned he could not conceal a look of bewilderment.

"They never heard of us at the university," he said. "I finally got the ROTC commander on the phone and he said he would send a truck out to pick us up. But they have no orders on us at all."

Tech-Sergeant Gnann swore in his soft Georgia accent. "Why, I could have taken you all home with me to Savannah for a couple of weeks."

"Hell, we could have all gone home!" said the Boy from Brooklyn. "The way this ASTP is fouled up they wouldn't have missed us until the war was over."

"Too late now," said Sergeant Sims.

After an hour or so, an old pre-war Army truck came chattering up to the platform and a gray-haired sergeant in faded khakis climbed out to stare at us. "Where'd you guys come from?" he asked.

We told him, and then filled the back of his truck with barracks bags and piled in on top of them. We rattled through the streets of Philadelphia, our rifles at the ready, watching the startled expressions on civilians' faces as we passed them, and then suddenly we were inside a big courtyard with the brick-walled dormitories of the University of Pennsylvania all around us. An aging pasty-faced captain, also in faded khakis, appeared out of a small building and watched us unload. Sergeant Sims hastily got us into formation, saluted, and reported.

"Stand at ease," the captain said. "Where did you say you men came from?"

"Auburn, sir, STAR center."

"Where the hell is that?"

"Alabama." Sims presented his big manila envelope.

The ROTC captain pulled out our orders and regarded them bleakly. "We have some ASTP units here," he said. "Area studies, medicine, and Arabic. But no setup for personnel psychologists. I've talked with the dean of students and he's assigned you the third floor of that dormitory over there." He pointed across the courtyard.

The building was old and ivy-covered, and while we were moving up to the third floor about thirty male civilian students— displaced by our unexpected arrival—were moving down to crowd in with some of their fellows on the lower levels. As we passed on the narrow stairway we regarded each other with mutual distrust. Later we discovered that most of these students were 4-Fs or ROTC men awaiting calls to officers' school.

By late afternoon we were settled into our quarters, my roommate being an earnest young PFC from Long Island who had just entered a New York law school when he was drafted. The rooms were adequate but not nearly so bright and cheery as those in the girls' dormitory at Auburn.

From Sergeant Sims we learned that since we were unassigned we would not join the other ASTP units for retreat, but that as soon as the ceremonies were over we could come down and follow them to the mess hall. Having had no food since leaving the John Jay that morning, we watched the retreat ceremonies with considerable impatience and wasted no time in falling in at the rear of the thousand or so ASTP students who marched out of the quadrangle. We formed into a platoon, and after marching in route formation for about a quarter of a mile we reached a large Horn & Hardart cafeteria which had been leased by the Army. The food lacked the character of the Auburn dining room, and we missed the pretty waitresses in their white dresses. To enjoy it, however, we had only to think back to the training camp mess halls and chow lines in the rain that we had left behind us a few weeks before.

But for the vigilance of Sergeant Sims, we probably would have missed breakfast the next morning. As it was, we barely made it out of the dormitory in time to bring up the rear of the six o'clock march to Horn & Hardart's. For the first time since entering the Army, we left our beds unmade and our rooms in disarray.

When we returned we found two charwomen busily mopping the hallway. They nodded politely to us as we trooped into our rooms to discover everything neatly arranged and the beds made up in civilian style. "My God," said my astonished roommate, "I'll bet that's the first time in the history of the U.S. Army that GI's had their beds made up by maids."

Bill Daley, a tech-four from Buffalo, New York, who occupied the adjoining room, stuck his head in the door. "Keep quiet about it, fellows. Loose lips sink battleships. So long as we don't talk about this, maybe we'll have maid service forever."

About nine o'clock, we were summoned down to the ROTC captain's office for a conference. We crowded into the small room, most of us sitting on the floor, while he regarded us gloomily from behind his battered desk.

"The university is getting nowhere in its efforts to identify your unit," he said. "We have attempted several times to reach someone by telephone in Washington who can help us, but apparently no one in the War Department has ever heard of you. We have also telephoned Auburn, and they insist that you are under orders to report to the University of Pennsylvania. We believe there is a foul-up somewhere. Most likely you have been sent to the wrong university." He leaned forward, touching the tips of his fingers together. "In the meantime, my responsibility is to keep you occupied. This morning you will police the grounds of the quadrangle. Sergeant Sims, when this duty is completed, report back to me."

For the next hour we fanned out over the grass of the quadrangle, searching vainly for cigarette butts and gum wrappers. I believe someone did find a fragment of a newspaper that probably had blown in from the street, but after all, every man in ASTP had learned to fieldstrip his cigarettes and ball his gum wrappers. That quadrangle must have been the cleanest piece of real estate in Philadelphia. At ten o'clock Sims called us together and suggested we make one more slow reconnaissance; if we completed our work too quickly, it was possible that the ROTC commander might have a more onerous assignment for us.

When Sims reported back, the captain had passes into Philadelphia ready for us. The passes expired at five P.M., at which time we were to be assembled in the quad with the other ASTP units for retreat ceremonies.

For the next few days, this daily routine continued. After breakfast each morning we policed the spotless quadrangle. The civilian students on the lower floors of our dorm eventually took pity on us and occasionally smashed a beer bottle in the guttering or tossed out a few cigarette butts for us to pick up. By ten every morning, however, we usually had our passes in hand and were off for downtown Philadelphia.

After about a week of this, the captain startled us one morning by issuing us a batch of ASTP shoulder patches to replace the varied insignia we wore on our sleeves. "You're not officially in ASTP yet," the captain muttered, "but we've had complaints from the military police. Some of you fellows are wearing shoulder patches of outfits which are already overseas."

With razor blades, needles, and thread we went to work, and by lunchtime our uniforms were ready to tell the world that we were soldiering with the ASTP. The shoulder emblem, which must have been rather hastily designed by an amateur artist in the Pentagon, was supposed to be a lamp of learning, but because of its shape an irreverent member of the organization quickly dubbed it "the Flaming Pisspot." My own unassigned group of twenty-five men was already known as the Goon Squad, and now we could further identify ourselves as the Goon Squad of the Flaming Pisspots.

This gave us a sense of belonging again, yet at times we suffered feelings of guilt. Even though we seldom saw a newspaper or listened to radio news, we knew that bloody battles were underway in Sicily. Some of us had trained with young men who were dying there. Yet there was no way to transfer out of ASTP even if we had wanted to do so to assuage our feelings of guilt. Sergeant Sims and two or three others had made serious inquiries about returning to their original units but were immediately rebuffed with a reply which became standard: *The assignment you are engaged upon is of such vital importance to the U.S. Army that transfer to another unit is not permissible.*

In the case of the Goon Squad, of course, our vital assignment consisted only of that daily sweep of the quadrangle and afternoons off in downtown Philadelphia. As the charwomen continued to make our beds and clean our rooms, we did not have even that soldierly duty to occupy our time, nor did we ever have to stand inspections. Because we had no physical training program, all of us were beginning to get out of shape.

Our biggest problem was lack of money. The Army payroll records had not caught up with us since we left the Southern training camps, and for three months none of us had received any money. We borrowed back and forth from each other until there was nothing left to exchange. Our one affluent member, the PFC of Independent Means who claimed to be a poet, paid the entire group's way into several movies. He also offered to lend us money individually, but not being sure just how independently wealthy he was, we declined to go in debt to him. To ease the money problem, our kindly ROTC captain obtained free passes to baseball games and other athletic events, and we soon found places in Philadelphia where men in uniform were made welcome. In that second year of World War II, a serviceman could obtain a drink by simply stepping up to any bar that was frequented by civilians. Some patriotic or guilt-ridden civilian would instantly offer to buy him a beer.

If we wearied of free beer, we had only to drop in to the Stagedoor Canteen, the Kitty Foyle Club, or one of the places run by various churches for servicemen. They would press sandwiches and healthful potables upon us. The Stagedoor Canteen became our favorite gathering place. It was populated by wealthy society girls from Philadelphia's Main Line who worked as hostesses. Unfortunately, they did not begin appearing at the Canteen until late in the afternoon—just about the time we had to head back to the university for five o'clock retreat ceremonies. We soon learned that we were missing all kinds of wonderful evening entertainment provided by America's leading performers, as well as several hours' companionship with the loveliest young ladies of Philadelphia.

It did not require much persuasion to send Sergeant Sims with a petition to the paternal ROTC captain, and to our great delight our daily passes were extended to midnight. Those of us who were willing to miss the evening mess at Horn & Hardart's no longer had to report back on the campus for retreat. Not a member of the Goon Squad who had a midnight pass in his pocket ever returned for retreat. The free sandwiches available may not have been as nutritious as Horn & Hardart's balanced meals, but the female companionship more than made up for the deficiency.

From that time on, the Stagedoor Canteen was the Goon Squad's home away from home. In addition to the companionship of pretty girls and free entertainment, there were quiet places where we could read. Several of us read long books which we had been unable to find time for before. To this day I associate *War and Peace*, *Don Quixote*, and *The Idiot* with Philadelphia's Stagedoor Canteen.

The only times we deserted the place were the evenings when male crooners such as Frank Sinatra—then a very frail young man—would show up. The girls had no time for us on those evenings; they devoted all their energies to intercepting the crooners, trying to snatch their buttons and neckties, or even just touching their sleeves. On those occasions we walked out in a body and went over to the Kitty Foyle Club, which was named after the working-girl heroine of Christopher Morley's popular novel about Philadelphia. The hostesses at the Kitty Foyle Club were just as attractive as those at the Stagedoor Canteen, but they were forever engaging us in Ping-Pong matches and other simple games, which they usually won, and the place lacked the glamour of the Stagedoor Canteen. As Bill Daley put it, the girls reminded him too much of those he had dated back home in Buffalo.

The rules of the Stagedoor Canteen forbade the young hostesses to make dates with servicemen who came there, but rules are made only to be broken. Usually some of the girls would arrange to leave early, and it was no coincidence that the Goon Squad would also leave early to stroll in a group down Walnut Street. We would appear to be surprised when two or three big shiny automobiles pulled up alongside and cheery feminine voices called out: "Can we offer you a lift, soldiers?"

Some evenings in Philadelphia between the hours of ten and midnight almost the entire membership of the Goon Squad would be dispersed among the mansions of Philadelphia's Main Liners. And then like male Cinderellas, as the hour of midnight approached, we were whisked in sleek automobiles back to the portals of the Pennsylvania University campus. As we trudged across the manicured quad, we could see lights in the crowded dormitories where our luckless fellows of the Flaming Pisspots sweated over their lessons in chemistry, mathematics, geography, and exotic languages of the Eastern world.

This sweet life came to an abrupt ending one summer morning when our ROTC captain informed us that we would no longer have daytime passes off the campus. He was turning us over to the university's football coaches, who evidently were as hard up as we were for something to keep them busy.

We reported to the football coaches that morning at eight o'clock, and for the next seven hours they kept us in constant motion. We ran, we jumped, we marched, we swam, we jogged, we climbed ropes, we went through every calisthenic routine known to man. That evening we could have had passes into town, but our bodies—softened by weeks of easy living—felt as if they had been run through a concrete mixer. Most of us were in our bunks by sundown.

For a couple of weeks we received the standard treatment then being given to University of Pennsylvania football recruits. Soon, to our surprise, we could jog five miles up and down the banks of the

Schuylkill River and finish in a fast dash without even breathing hard. And then we were spending our evenings again at the Stagedoor Canteen.

About this time, a new commandant suddenly arrived on the scene. We had been vaguely aware of a steadily growing contingent of students known as V-12s—the Navy's counterpart of the Army's ASTP—who were quartered somewhere on the opposite side of the campus. The V-12 and ASTP units together now numbered about three thousand men, and to control this sprawling aggregation, an aging colonel of a boys' military academy was summoned from retirement.

Our ROTC captain introduced him to us one morning at the first combined Army–Navy reveille ceremony. From the vantage point of the Goon Squad's position just to the left of the wooden platform where he stood, we could see the colonel quite clearly. He was in brand-new summer khakis which probably would have fit him twenty years earlier, but he could no longer stand upright to his full six feet and his flesh had shrunk to his bones. Consequently his blouse sagged and his trousers drooped so that he resembled an ancient scarecrow with the head of a corded-necked old lion protruding from the top of the uniform.

"Lads," his voice screeched out of the loud speakers, "I just want to tell you it's a good feeling to be back in harness. You lads are all engaged here at this great university in brain work which may determine the outcome of this war. Although you are not in combat, discipline is of first importance here as on the battlefield."

To emphasize his points the old colonel slapped his hands together in front of the microphone, each time making a sound like an explosion and drowning out his key words. The point of his little introductory speech was to inform us that we lads must shape up, and to expedite matters he had prepared a mimeographed sheet of instructions which our platoon leaders would pick up and distribute to us. We were to follow these instructions in the arrangement of our quarters, and before we fell out for each morning's formation, every room must be ready for inspection. A system of demerits based on our personal appearance, behavior, and the condition of our quarters would thenceforth determine the issuance of passes off the campus.

After we returned from breakfast, Sergeant Sims brought us the mimeographed sheets, and we all gathered in his room for a discussion of this threat to our liberties and our pursuit of happiness at the Stagedoor Canteen. Naturally we were all highly indignant. Sims grinned sheepishly as he passed out the instructions. "I'm supposed to read this to you," he drawled. "By God, it's the same stuff they gave me when I went to military academy at the age of twelve."

The first part of the instructions was a series of little homilies about keeping regular hours, regular toilet schedules, bathing, deep breathing, avoiding thoughts about sex, and making certain the windows were open before going to bed so that we would enjoy the benefits of fresh air. (In Philadelphia on steamy summer nights we had learned to close the windows to keep out the fetid air.) This was followed by lists of weighted demerits based on everything from dust on the windowpanes to comic books in footlockers. (We had no footlockers.) At the bottom was a diagram representing two layers of a footlocker marked off in little squares, each labeled for some article of clothing. Handkerchiefs, socks, underwear, shirts, etc. had to be placed in these exact positions. As in army barracks, shoes were to be placed at one end of the bed, and beds must be made up military style with sheets folded back over blankets tight enough to bounce a silver dollar.

We commented profanely as we studied these information sheets, and Bill Daley remarked that it was worse than the real Army, but we all knew better than that. What we wanted was to protect our evening passes, and the next morning we had items arranged in our bureau drawers exactly as the old colonel diagrammed them for footlockers. We had our spare shoes shined like mirrors and properly positioned under beds, and for the first time since our arrival at the university we made up our beds—military style, of course.

On returning from breakfast we received quite a shock. The good charwomen had come in while we were gone and had moved all our shoes into closets and remade the beds in comfortable civilian style. Praying that the colonel had not visited us while we were away, we hurried downstairs to where the charwomen were cleaning the civilian students' rooms.

No, they had seen no one inspecting our rooms. Yes, they would henceforth leave everything exactly as we left it, but surely we would want them to continue cleaning and sweeping. If we reported that we did not need charwomen, they said, one of them would likely lose her job. We made a deal with them; we would say nothing if they would say nothing, and every morning they would dust our windowpanes carefully.

Much relieved, we marched off to report to the football coaches.

The weather was extremely hot and humid in Philadelphia that summer, and the hard training and continual sweating made all of us lean and iron-muscled. Not one of the Goons had ever played college football, and I doubt if any of us could have made a regular team, but there were few regular teams left anywhere in that second year of the war. The coaches began talking about the possibilities of forming a sort of unofficial university team from our twenty-five-man squad. They gave us practice in some contact plays, and we began dreaming of taking on Army or Navy or some other real team when autumn came.

We reckoned without the old colonel, however. In his thorough way he had pored over the ASTP records and found the Goon Squad. Unbeknown to us, he had called in the ROTC captain and demanded to know why we were not attending classes. The captain explained as best he could that the War Department in Washington was still trying to locate our orders, and that as soon as this was done we would be transferred to the proper university for training as personnel psychologists. This did not satisfy the colonel. If there were no ASTP classes for us, then we should attend summer classes with civilian students. After thrashing about among various deans, the colonel arranged for us to start classes at the beginning of the late summer session—only one week away when we learned about it.

We spent most of the week's reprieve in mourning. We mourned, the football coaches mourned, the pretty hostesses at the Stagedoor Canteen mourned for us. We all knew that nothing could be done about it, however. Fortunately for us, perhaps, in the middle of the gloomy week our minds were taken off our fate when the Goon Squad became the leading participants in a strange and exciting event.

The morning it began, Sergeant Sims received orders to bring the entire squad down to the ROTC captain's office. As we filed into the small room we were surprised to see the old colonel waiting there, his wrinkled lion's face appearing very grim.

"Lads," he began, "I see from your records that most of you completed basic combat training before being chosen for the important brain work you are doing here. I'd like a show of hands from those of you who have been through firing range practice."

All of us raised our hands.

He beamed. "Excellent. Now, how many of you have fired the good old Springfield rifle?"

This time only about a dozen of us raised our hands; the others had fired only the M-1.

The colonel nodded to the captain. "I think they will be sufficient, a good dozen or so. Sergeant, take the names of that last group. That will be all, lads. Thank you."

As we marched off to the football field, we tried to unravel the meaning of that brief scene. All of us who had fired the Springfield regretted having held up our hands. We were wary of the old colonel, wary of the Army power he represented. The Boy from Brooklyn tried to start a rumor that someone had been court-martialed and we were to be the firing squad. We almost believed him.

Late that evening, Sergeant Sims came around and ordered those of us who were in the Springfield rifle squad to prepare our leggings, cartridge belts, and helmets for inspection. If any of these items were not included in our issued equipment we would have to go with him to the ROTC armory and draw them. Most of us still had field equipment stored away in our barracks bags, but we had not worn leggings, belts, and helmets for so long they seemed strange to us.

"What's this all about?" I asked.

"You know as much as I do," Sims replied.

Next morning before sunrise, the Springfield rifle squad assembled in the ROTC office, with orders not to show ourselves outside until after reveille ceremonies were over. During the long wait we ate cold sandwiches and drank tepid coffee that had been brought in for us. After a while we could hear the sounds of reveille on the quad, and a few minutes later the old colonel appeared in the office. He carried his lion head higher than usual on his corded neck, and he seemed charged with energy.

"Well, lads," he said, rubbing his hands together and then slapping them sharply, "we have important work before us this morning. Sergeant, issue arms and ammunition!"

Sims led us over to a table where a dozen Springfield rifles that looked old enough to have been used in the Civil War lay waiting for us. As we passed by we chose one, and Sims handed each of us two .30 caliber cartridges.

"Now, lads," the colonel said, "I want you to load one of those cartridges and place the other in your cartridge belt. Make certain you know exactly where that spare cartridge is in case you should need to reload in a hurry. Are you all sure you know how to reload quickly?" We were making quite a racket testing the noisy bolts. "You, son," the colonel cried, pointing to the Historian in our group. "Let me see you eject and reload that cartridge."

The Historian was slow and awkward. Sergeant Sims's face paled as the barrel of the loaded rifle swept around the room. We all had to go through the loading test, and it was a miracle that none of us pulled a trigger in our nervousness. We were beginning to wonder if the Boy from Brooklyn was right, that we *had* been selected as a firing squad for an execution.

From the narrow drive outside came an unexpected roar of motors, and through slits in the window blinds we could see four big black limousines drawing up. The colonel hurried outside. We could not hear what he was saying, but one of the dark-suited drivers got out and began removing small blue flags which bore the name of a Philadelphia funeral parlor. All this seemed quite ominous to us.

In a minute or so, the colonel returned. He glanced at his watch. "Twelve and a half minutes to H-Hour, lads. Check your leggings and belts and put on helmets. Sergeant, form them in single file at the door. Three men will enter each car, one in front with the driver, two in the rear. Remember to carry rifles at port arms as you march out."

As luck would have it, I drew the rear car, the one the old colonel chose to ride in. Sergeant Sims rode in the front seat, and the colonel sat between me and the Boy from Brooklyn. I held my rifle upright between my knees.

Throbbing with repressed power, the big black limousines crawled out of the portals of the campus and then went skimming down Woodland Avenue. After glancing nervously back through the rear window, the colonel relaxed with a sigh. "So far, so good." He slapped my knee and my rifle muzzle jarred against the low roof of the limousine, the barrel almost knocking off my steel helmet. "Well, lads, I suppose I should have arranged for a police motorcycle escort, but I didn't want to attract any attention." As it was, every civilian we passed gave us a double take when they saw a procession of black limousines carrying helmeted soldiers bristling with rifles.

A few minutes later, we were deep into downtown Philadelphia, slowing to a stop-and-go speed in heavy traffic. Then suddenly we turned a corner and the cars pulled into the curb where NO PARKING AT ANY TIME signs were spaced every few yards.

"Out, out!" the colonel cried. I stepped out and offered my free hand to help his bony frame from the rear seat, but he refused indignantly. "No, lad. Stand at attention! Port arms! Port arms!" he repeated as I pulled the rifle off my shoulder.

He went trotting off down the sidewalk, the loose sleeves of his blouse flapping. In his querulous old man's voice he began shouting to other members of the Springfield rifle squad to get out on the sidewalk. We were in an unfamiliar part of Philadelphia on a short street of tall office buildings with conservative gold-lettered signs of legal firms, brokerage houses, banks, and insurance companies indicating that it must be the financial district.

After stationing armed men at each corner of the street and along the sidewalk, the colonel posted two guards in front of a dark-glassed entrance and then led the remaining four of us inside. As we hurried up a wide curving flight of stairs to the second floor, he turned suddenly to me. "You, lad, drop back and take post on the stair landing. Don't let anybody come up or down these steps until I return."

"Yes, sir," I said. I stood there awkwardly on the broad landing, absolutely alone with my trusty Springfield. There were no sounds except for a rising hubbub of street voices coming muffled through the closed entrance doors. The heavy steel combat helmet pressed down on my skull and I could feel the faint beginnings of a headache.

Then from the hallway above me I heard the tapping of heels on marble flooring. A dark-haired girl with legs like Betty Grable's swung into view. She put one high-heeled foot down on the second step and then froze there, staring at me in dumb surprise. She moved the other lovely leg tentatively, and then I remembered the colonel's orders. "You can't come down, Miss," I said.

"Why are you standing there?" she demanded.

"I can't answer that, Miss."

"Then I'm coming down." She took two more steps and I assumed the combat position as taught by my basic training sergeant—legs spread, Springfield at the ready. She kept coming and I raised the rifle. She screamed and ran back up the steps, vanishing from my sight, but I could hear the tapping of her racing heels merging into the steady tread of heavier feet.

The colonel, the three men he had taken with him, and two white-shirted civilians came quickly into view. They were carrying large canvas bags, very heavy bags to judge by the straining arms of the carriers. I sprang to attention, port arms, the colonel frowning at me as he staggered past under his load. "Son, you frightened that young lady," he scolded, and then added: "Fall in behind and cover us."

We moved out onto the sidewalk in the glare of the summer morning. Traffic was stalled and hordes of people milled everywhere. When he saw the crowds gathering around the limousines, the colonel almost dropped his canvas bag. "God!" was all he could say. We pushed through to our car. A woman was shoved against me. "Are they spies?" she asked in a hoarse voice, pointing toward the two civilians who were efficiently stowing the bags in the car trunk. The Boy from Brooklyn answered, his voice mimicking hers: "No, ma'am, they merely robbed a bank."

Somehow we all managed to get back in the cars, which began

crawling slowly through the mob. The people's faces, which had been filled with excited curiosity, now showed signs of anger because no one had told them why we were there, and they realized the secret reason for our presence was escaping from them so that they would never know. A man banged both hands on the window next to me, his eyes imploring me to tell him something, anything, and then the car jerked forward. We swung around the corner and moved swiftly away.

"God!" the old colonel repeated as he mopped his sweating brow. "People can smell money, I tell you, lads. What else could have brought all those people there? I did everything I could think of not to attract attention—plain black cars instead of Army vehicles, no police with their noisy sirens, just a few ordinary soldier boys. They smelled that money, I tell you."

Now that I was fairly certain we were not going to be used as a firing squad, I felt relieved. Guarding money was nothing compared to shooting a blindfolded traitor or a spy.

"Something over half a million dollars we're sitting right on top of, lads. What do you think of that?"

"Sir," the Boy from Brooklyn asked politely, "would I be out of line if I asked where we're taking it?"

"Of course not, son. Right back to the university. It's our payroll. I understand that most of you lads haven't been paid for three or four months."

"Yes, sir, the Goon Squad is four months over."

A loud report like a rifle shot brought the old colonel upright. It was a backfire from a motorcycle that came chattering alongside us. The husky cyclist wore a greasy undershirt, and his muscular arms were blue with tattoos. A bleached blonde in tight white shorts was glued against his back. The cyclist appeared to be very excited. He shouted something, but his words were drowned out by the continuous backfiring of his old motorcycle. The colonel leaned over me to wave him away, but the cyclist misunderstood and pulled in so close I could see the gold in his teeth.

"Where're the German parachutists?" he yelled.

"Did he say parachutists?" the colonel asked me.

"German parachutists, I think, sir."

"He's a lunatic. Let down your window, son!" The colonel leaned across me again, his bony elbow and the Springfield rifle digging into my stomach. "There are no German parachutists!" the colonel yelled. The rush of air blew his words back into the car. He thrust his head out the window: "Go away!"

The cyclist raised a fist. "We'll get them damned Nazis!" he replied.

"Go away!" the colonel repeated.

The bleached blonde gave the colonel an erotic red-lipped smile, keeping her face turned back as the cyclist gunned his old machine forward, making his way to the head of the procession to escort us to the University of Pennsylvania, where he finally was forced to abandon us.

For the next thirty-six hours, the Goons' Springfield rifle squad stood guard duty in the armory while a couple of paymasters from Washington doled out precise amounts of cash to three thousand money-hungry soldiers and sailors. The Goons were the last to be paid, of course, and by that time it was past midnight and too late to go to the Stagedoor Canteen.

The following Monday we were entered as students in the university's summer session.

Attending classes with civilians had a sobering effect upon us, especially after the old colonel sent signed letters to each member of the Goon Squad, informing us that the grades we made in summer school would determine whether or not we would eventually become personnel psychology students within ASTP. Our classes included zoology, math, geography, semantics, and basic psychology. We also met twice a week with the ROTC captain, who reindoctrinated us with all the old Army films we had seen in basic training, including the ever-popular sex hygiene movie. In the civilian classes we were segregated, being seated in the rear or to one side of the classrooms the way blacks were once segregated in theaters and other public places. We felt like untouchables when the instructors carefully explained to the civilian students that we would be graded separately from them and therefore would not be in competition with them for A's.

Had it not been for a timid little girl who served as a lab assistant, the zoology course would have been a bore with its notebook drawings and the inevitable surgical work on frogs. We had been through all that in high school and college and had no enthusiasm for a third time around. After the instructor assigned this shy young girl scientist to the military section of the class, however, the lab sessions became more endurable. She evidently had seen no soldiers at close range before and must have believed all the legendary stories she had read or heard about rape and pillage associated with invading armies. Our uniforms awed her and our language shocked her, especially the double entendres that flowed from the lips of the Goons while they were dissecting frogs. Each day we expected her to break down under our verbal cruelties, but she doggedly endured us and gradually learned to insult us with a deadly coolness for our zoological stupidities. Before the summer session ended we were all in love with her.

The Amateur Psychologist of our group had nothing good to say about the basic psychology course. "They haven't introduced anything new here since the days of William James," he remarked several times. I found the course entertaining, however, with its lively demonstrations. During a series of memory tests, an idiot with a photographic memory and a moron with similar auditory recall outdid all of us, and this had a shattering effect upon our Amateur Psychologist, which I felt he deserved.

The days went swiftly by. Highly motivated by our desire to remain in ASTP and out of the infantry, we studied late into the nights, and on weekends we often cut short our visits to the Stagedoor Canteen in order to get back to the dormitory to keep up with class assignments. We noticed that the days were growing shorter, the shadows longer, the nights cooler. Autumn was coming, and we heard optimistic reports about the war. Sicily was won, Italy was cracking up, and the Japanese were on the run in the Pacific. We wondered if it would not all be over before we ever got into that personnel psychology program.

One evening, about two weeks before the summer session was scheduled to end, Sergeant Sims made the rounds to inform us that the ROTC captain wanted us all down in his office. "What's up?"

everybody asked, but Sims didn't know. On the way down, the Boy from Brooklyn quickly spread a dozen rumors but we discounted all of them. Perhaps the War Department had found our orders, at last, and the captain was going to make a ceremony of giving us the details of our new destination. Everybody picked his favorite university out of the air—Harvard, Yale, Princeton, Stanford.

We trooped gaily into the office and made ourselves comfortable on the floor. "Smoke if you like," the captain said, his voice too kind. The sympathy in it made us nervous.

As soon as we were all settled, he stood up and braced himself by placing his hands down upon the desk. "I'm not going to beat around the bush," he began. "As you know, you have only two more weeks of classes. When summer school ends, your stay at the University of Pennsylvania ends. We simply don't have anything else for you to do here."

We sat there speechless, unbelieving. My mind went back to a summer when I'd struggled to get a job with a construction outfit and then after a few days work, a foreman made a similar speech just before firing all his new employees. The captain sounded exactly like that construction foreman: "We're going to have to let you go, fellows. Fact of the matter is, you're unemployed in the Army."

We laughed but there was no humor in the sound of it. The captain continued: "I like you boys and want to give you a break. If you can find a job somewhere in the Army, we'll see that you get sent there at War Department expense. If your original outfit is still stateside and you wish to go back to it, we'll help you find it. Otherwise we must send you to a reception center for reassignment wherever they may be able to place you."

We all knew that would be the infantry, and we wanted none of it. For the next twenty-four hours, the Goons spent every spare moment telephoning or writing letters that were sent special delivery—hoping desperately to solve our individual unemployment problems before the Army solved them for us.

Some weeks earlier my understanding wife, Sally—who was working in a defense office in Washington—had informed me that she had met a colonel in Army Ground Forces who was searching for enlisted men who had been reference librarians in civilian life.

At the time I had dismissed any hope of obtaining such an assignment because of ASTP's adamant rule against transfers; besides, I had learned to like the Flaming Pisspots and did not wish to leave them. The situation was now altered, however, and after persuading the ROTC captain that I needed a one-day pass to Washington to find military employment there, I took off for the capital.

It was late in the day before I finally tracked down the colonel who was interested in librarians. He was in a remote section of Washington on a small peninsula jutting out into the Potomac where the Army War College had operated in peacetime. When World War II began, the Ground Forces took it over as their headquarters.

Like most of the other officers I had seen since leaving the 80th Division, the colonel was past retirement age. He was a small man, his close-cropped white hair thinning a bit and his sun-tanned skin stretching like parchment over his facial bones. He seemed glad to see me and explained that he was in command of some kind of information service that required a great deal of research to answer the tough questions being thrown at him. He had been desperately attempting to find former reference librarians among enlisted men but discovered that the Army classified librarians as educators so that they had become lost among all the former schoolteachers. I didn't tell him that I had been classified as a farmer.

As soon as I'd outlined my civilian experience, he assured me that I was just the sort of enlisted man he wanted, and he immediately called in a sergeant to take my name, rank, and serial number. The colonel had never heard of ASTP, but he accepted my explanation that our assignment at the University of Pennsylvania was completed and that a transfer would be authorized on receipt of a request from Army Ground Forces Headquarters. I added that unless the transfer request was received in two weeks the university would be shipping me out to a reception center for reassignment. He promised to expedite the request for my transfer.

Feeling well pleased with myself, I walked back through the tree-shaded Army post, past a row of rambling old houses with the names of generals and colonels above each entranceway, and then along the galleried front of the enlisted men's white-washed brick building. With its air of the nineteenth century, the place reminded me of old army posts I'd seen on the Western plains, and I was sure I was going to be happy there.

After a joyous celebration with Sally, I returned to Philadelphia. When I arrived the Goons were also celebrating because one of our members had just received confirmation of his transfer to an Army detachment in Florida with headquarters in a Miami hotel that had been taken over by the Air Force. I announced my similar good fortune, and the merrymaking continued into the night.

We were still required to attend classes, but the motivation to study had vanished. Two or three days after my trip to Washington, the Goons were assembled in a small psychology laboratory to perform a series of experiments. Our lab instructor, a bored middle-aged man who hated his job, handed each of us a small hammer device with a needle point attached to a lead weight, and also a card with an outline of a human hand marked off in sections. We were supposed to take turns pecking at each others' hands, and if we felt a cold sensation we entered a *C* in the proper space on the card. If we felt a hot sensation we wrote in an *H*.

There we were, a roomful of adult males of sound minds and bodies, wearing uniforms of the U.S. Army, pecking away with those absurd little hammers at each others' hands when the door opened and a cherubic-faced major entered quietly. He peered at us for a moment, his eyes puzzled, his mouth twisting in a repressed grin. "Is this Sergeant Sims's squad?"

Sims arose and assumed responsibility for us.

In a soft voice the major identified himself as an emissary from Special Service Forces in Washington, and then without preliminaries informed us that the War Department had found our missing orders. We would be receiving transfer orders within twenty-four hours.

Four days later, the Goons were in a ramshackle dormitory hard by the Iowa River, which flows through the campus of the University of Iowa, in Iowa City, Iowa. For the first time now we were inside the real world of ASTP, a world that had grown so sophisticated at the University of Iowa that we were offered opportunities to buy Flaming Pisspot rings and pins. Already the Lamp of Learning adorned notebook covers, and we discovered there was an official ASTP song that we were supposed to sing—to the tune of the Notre Dame fight song—as we marched from one class to another:

Hail! Hail to ASTP
Why did this ever happen to me?
Physics, English, Chem and Math
Not even time to take a bath.

There were many bawdy versions, of course, as well as a tearful ballad, only one verse of which I remember:

Take down your service flag, mother,
Your son is in the ASTP.

We began our training with about a dozen written examinations, virtually the same as those we had endured at Auburn months before. After this was over, a lieutenant gave us a speech in which he informed us that if we survived the personnel psychology program we would be assigned to a special section that would aid young men being discharged from the Army in finding their proper pursuits in civilian life. "This means," he said flatly, "that you yourselves will be among the very last men to be discharged after the war ends. I think I can promise you that you will be rewarded for your patience, however, by being commissioned lieutenants. If any of you wish to withdraw from such a prospect, you must do so immediately."

No one withdrew. We now entered upon a grueling crash program of classes that ran from eight A.M. to five P.M. without a break except for lunch. Organized study hours were from six P.M. to midnight.

I took none of this seriously, arising every morning in full confidence that the day would bring my transfer orders to Army Ground Forces Headquarters. At last I received an official communication direct from the white-haired colonel. In substance the letter was a reprimand, Paragraph 1 demanding to know why I had come to Washington and misrepresented my availability, Paragraph 2 quoting a reply the colonel had received from ASTP headquarters: "Request for transfer of enlisted man denied because the assignment

he is engaged upon is of vital importance to the U.S. Army."
Paragraph 3 consisted of a curt statement ordering me to reply by
endorsement, explaining my unmilitary conduct.

Fearing imminent court-martial, I carefully composed an endorsement to the letter. In the cold dead style of military communicators, I informed the colonel that I had not misrepresented
my availability at the time I visited him and went on to explain how
my situation had unexpectedly changed. I then wound up with a
brief one-sentence apology for wasting his time. When I dropped
the letter in the mailbox, I believed it would save me from a court-
martial and that I would never hear again from AGF headquarters.

Surrendering myself to a career in the Army as a personnel
psychologist rather than a librarian, I devoted all my energies to the
sixteen-hours-a-day classroom and study program. Just as I was
growing accustomed to the routine, I received a sudden summons
one morning to appear at the headquarters of the Iowa unit's commanding officer. When I arrived there, I found another ASTP soldier
already in the waiting room. A few moments later both of us were
shown into the commander's office.

"Good morning, men," he said. "We have some extraordinary
news for you. For the first time since we organized this ASTP unit,
we've been ordered to release two of our assignees. You men certainly must have some very special kind of know-how. I congratu-
late you." He reached across his desk, presented us with our travel
orders, and gravely shook our hands. "You will be leaving Iowa City
early this afternoon. Good luck, men."

As I walked out of the office half-stunned, wondering how the
white-haired little colonel in Army Ground Forces had managed to
pull off a miracle, I asked my companion where he was going.

"Can't tell you specifically," he replied. "Highly secret location. I'm a radar scientist, you know. Should never have been
drafted, and certainly should have never been put in ASTP. They've
had the devil of a time getting me out of here."

At that time in the war, radar was very mysterious and very
secret, and I properly expressed my admiration for his scientific
genius.

"And you," he asked, giving me a supercilious glance. "What's your new assignment?"

"AGF HQ. Reference librarian," I said, feeling pretty damned proud to be the representative of a profession that the War Department had come to esteem as highly as radar science.

For several weeks after I reported for duty in Washington, I exchanged short letters with a few members of the Goon Squad. Life for the Goons, I learned, had turned uncharacteristically gray out there in Iowa; the suspense and excitement, the daffiness and joie de vivre seemed to have vanished. Then with no advance warning, the Army abolished the entire ASTP, sucked its 150 thousand misfits into infantry regiments, and sped them to Europe. Many of them went into the 106th Division.

On a cold foggy morning in December, the German Army opened its last great offensive of the war. Pouring out of the Ardennes Forest, the full force of its armor struck the 106th Division. The green, poorly trained young men of the Flaming Pisspots suffered heavy casualties there.

When I first learned of this, I remembered the conversation late at night on the Pullman car John Jay as it rocked us over the rails toward Philadelphia and the University of Pennsylvania. *The army invented this ASTP to save the colleges from going bust,* our cynical Amateur Psychologist had said.

No, our Historian disagreed, ASTP *must have been devised to keep America's bright young men from dying in combat.*

And then the corporal from the New York garment district had scoffed: *Bright young men? We're just smart at passing tests. Nothing else.*

And there must end this footnote to the history of the Army Specialized Training Program, that forgotten assemblage of young men who wore the Lamp of Learning on their sleeves for a brief interval during World War II, the Flaming Pisspots who were smart at passing tests and nothing else.

CHAPTER ELEVEN

Caught in the Cold War

UNTIL THE END OF WORLD WAR II, I was assigned to Army Ground Forces Headquarters in Washington. Much of the time I worked for officers who were studying the voluminous reports that poured in from battlefields on all fronts around the world. Like the reference and research work done by civilian librarians, the duty sometimes was absorbing, even exciting, but sometimes it was monotonous. As an enlisted man I found that the higher the rank of an officer, the easier it was to work alongside him. The seasoned colonels, especially the West Pointers, recognized that I was a civilian who happened to be wearing a uniform. Most of them made clear and patient explanation about the information they were looking for—such as the performance of a specific weapon in combat—and they usually appeared to be satisfied with the results I brought them.

During this period, I formed an enduring friendship with a colleague, Martin Schmitt, who had also been a librarian in civilian life. One evening in the barracks I noticed that his footlocker was filled with books about the Old West. We immediately began talking about the classics on the subject—Josiah Gregg, Randolph Marcy, Lewis and Clark. He loved John Neihardt's heroic *Songs* about the Indian Wars and the fur-trapping Mountain Men and could recite stanzas from them. I soon discovered that Schmitt was a Western America fanatic like me.

After the war ended, we both had to remain in service for a few months until the point system of demobilization brought us to our discharges. Our official duties declined steadily, and during this waiting period we began collecting historical photographs of the Old West, mainly to pass the time. Some of our wartime assignments had made us familiar with the War Department's collection of photographs, and by chance we had discovered the old Indian Wars file. After choosing favorite photographs from this source we went on to the National Archives, Library of Congress, Bureau of American Ethnology and other government agencies to obtain more eight-by-ten-inch prints, mostly of American Indians. Before we realized it, we had a considerable collection between us and had expended most of our spare cash.

On Saturdays and Sundays when we manned the telephone desk (a duty that required less and less time), we studied our photographs, trying to improve on the identifications and dates. Schmitt was especially interested in the photographers and spent many of his off-duty hours in the Copyright Office tracking the glass-plate pioneers in the West.

We had given but little thought to putting our collection into a book, but this idea came suddenly into focus one day when an editor from Macmillan came to see us. He had traveled down from New York to investigate the possibilities of a heavily illustrated book on the American Indian Wars. He told us that everywhere he went around the government agencies in search of pictures he had been referred to us as collectors on the subject. He examined our photographs with evident excitement and asked if he could take them with him to New York. We were having none of that, however; our entire soldiers' capital was in that collection. We told him that we needed a week to arrange them in some sort of narrative form, and then one of us would bring them up to Macmillan.

I won the flip of a coin to determine who the messenger would be. In my sergeant's uniform, with a twenty-four-hour pass in my pocket, I spent an afternoon in the oak-lined offices of Macmillan and joined a group of editors around a long oaken table, drinking tea and showing off the photographs. The upshot of this was a decision a few weeks later by the Macmillan editors that the production of such a book would be too expensive to find a market. In the 1940s the engraving of photographs for printing was very costly.

Getting the book into print was a long and arduous process. The University of Oklahoma Press attempted to obtain a special grant to cover expenses but failed to do so, and after many months returned the photographs in rather poor condition. Not long after

Brown (left) with Jack Rogers and Martin Schmitt on the Potomac Appalachian Trail, 1945

that, a historian at the university published a history of the Indian wars, using as illustrations a number of the photographs we had collected.

By this time Schmitt and I were out of the army and back into civilian life. When Schmitt came east on vacation from his post on the West Coast, we decided to replace the damaged photographs and try to interest Charles Scribner's Sons, resolving that this would be our last effort to find a publisher. We knew that Scribner's had recently published a selection of Civil War photographs without going bankrupt.

Scribner's was enthusiastic from the beginning; Charles Scribner II wrote us a personal letter, wanting to see our collection. Because I was in the East while Schmitt was in the West, I had the pleasure of working closely with a pair of splendid editors, R.V. Coleman and Joe Hopkins. The only time of doubt about the book's fate was on the day I was summoned to New York for a final meeting that was to include a consultation with the famous Maxwell Perkins, who at that time made the final approval on every book published by Scribner's. I had never met nor seen him.

Before I was sent to Perkins's office, Coleman and Hopkins both warned me that he often turned off his hearing aid during conversations, but that I should answer all his questions to the point and make no comments about anything unless asked.

Perkins's office was a long room with several windows that had very wide sills. Along these windowsills and then around the edges of a large table, Perkins had placed in sequence the 270 eight-by-ten photographs, their typed captions beneath. With Perkins leading the way, we walked along the lines of photographs, he occasionally pointing down at one and asking a question. Three or four times he shifted the order of arrangement, glancing at me as if to demand my approval and saying something about a slight alteration of captions being necessary with the change of sequence.

At the very end, he stood erect and looked me straight in the eyes. "Where are the Navajos?" he demanded.

Somewhat lamely I explained that we had been unable to find enough Navajo photographs to fit the period and theme of our picture narrative. (Some years later the very photographs we had wanted suddenly appeared from some lost hiding place.)

Perkins looked unhappy over my reply. "The Navajos are my favorite tribe," he said. Then he shrugged, waved me out of his office, and turned toward his desk. "We'll make a fine book," he called after me. "Tell Coleman it's all right." That was my only meeting with Maxwell Perkins.

The book was published in 1948 under the title *The Fighting Indians of the West*. It remained in print for many years, and would be in print today had the printing films not been lost. Schmitt and I later collaborated on two other photographic histories, *The Settlers' West* and *Trail Driving Days,* both published by Scribner's

Creating a narrative from historical pictures, with captions and text, is a fascinating way to spend one's time but it is also very trying. I would never venture upon such an undertaking without a partner, and I highly recommend that all storytellers interested in such techniques first find a congenial and like-minded partner to share in the required travel, the numerous difficult decisions, and considerable costs.

After leaving the Army I was offered a post at the Aberdeen Proving Ground in Maryland, and I accepted because the pay was much better than my former job at the Beltsville Research Center. And it was needed because my family was increasing, with Mitchell already born and Linda on the way.

Although the Aberdeen Proving Ground was only sixty miles from Beltsville, the ambience was quite different, almost a total contrast in raison d'être, in subject matter, in attitudes. The proving ground's purpose was to test or "prove" guns, ammunition, and combat vehicles. During the two years I was there no one ever addressed me, or introduced me, as a librarian. I was the chief of a branch. To the military establishment, librarians are people who are responsible for collections of recreational reading matter. Military research libraries are usually given grandiose names such as Intelligence Service Commands or Scientific Communications Centers. My realm was the Technical Information Branch, or TIB.

When I decided to take the appointment, the Army was held in fairly high regard after the close of a war the nation had accepted as unavoidable. I thought we were through with wars practically forever, although I was aware that research on weapons would continue for prudence' sake. I looked forward to a pleasant, interesting, and peaceful time at Aberdeen as librarian—or chief, as my job description insisted. Unfortunately, I did not foresee the Cold War.

Winston Churchill's "iron curtain" speech at Fulton, Missouri, early in 1946 is often pointed to as the first public declaration of the Cold War. For me, that conflict actually began at the Aberdeen Proving Ground about that same time. I was occupied in reorganizing a fairly large collection of printed materials and an *enormous* collection of documents marked SECRET or CONFIDENTIAL. There were hundreds of thousands of these classified items stored in vaults and in locked files behind barred doors and windows. I had never in my life seen so many locks concentrated in one place. One of my duties was to maintain—in a secret place in a locked desk—a file of combinations to locks on the vault doors. Every Monday morning the combinations were changed, and then the new combinations were locked up until needed.

Except for the time-consuming aspects, none of this bothered me at first. With the help of an energetic captain assigned to assist us, we were engaged in declassifying much of the secret material. The captain and I were both naive enough to believe that eventually we would have *no* secret documents and could maintain an open library. After a few weeks we discovered that for every secret document that we declassified, at least a hundred *new* secret documents arrived for us to guard. The Army's research organization had not been reduced after the war ended, and energetic researchers all around the country churned out an unceasing flood of secret reports relating to weapons and matériel for future wars.

The military-industrial complex, which was involved with many of these secrets, would be brought into the open by President Eisenhower in 1961. Fifteen years before that speech, my awareness of the existence of this complex dawned at the first postwar demonstration of new weapons at Aberdeen. The colonel to whom I was responsible invited me to attend this demonstration with him.

He told me that I had been handling paper on the gadgets and it was time for me to see the real things being tested.

We rode out in a jeep to an open field at one end of which was a section of unroofed bleacher seats, and took our places among a crowd of well-dressed civilians and brilliantly uniformed officers. In front of us were several big guns facing a row of old tanks and bombing planes far out on the flats of Chesapeake Bay. While we waited, the colonel explained that the civilians present were ordnance manufacturers from various industrial cities, and that many of the uniformed officers were military observers from the embassies of friendly countries. He added that during the war, the Soviet Union had always sent the most observers but that there would be none of them there that day.

Just as I was on the point of asking why the Russians were not there, a big gun right in front of us blasted a missile into one of the distant tanks. The spectators cheered. For a long time the guns banged away, deafeningly, gradually destroying the tanks and airplanes. Sometimes the crowd cheered and sometimes it remained silent. For me, it was like watching a football game and not knowing the rules. Except for the total absence of women, the audience was much like a football crowd on a sunny autumn afternoon—laughing, smoking, drinking, and cheering when they were pleased with something, such as one of the rusty old bombing planes being ripped apart by a rocket.

Next morning, I noticed in a Baltimore newspaper a very brief item datelined Washington reporting that the Soviet embassy was protesting because their military observers had not been invited to the demonstration at Aberdeen. All that day—in the offices, during coffee breaks, in lunchrooms—the Russians were the main topic of conversation. The stories started out as jokes in the morning, but by noontime they had grown into sizable rumors about carloads of Russians appearing at the entrance gate and demanding to be admitted to the demonstration. By late afternoon I was hearing that the Russians had tried to use force to push their way past the military police. I was never able to find anyone who had actually seen any Russians, but the stories persisted for several days.

Whether there was a fragment of truth behind any of it I never knew, but the post's security division now began issuing memoranda ordering a tightening of security measures against what was quickly turning into the Cold War. Because my staff and I were responsible for hundreds of thousands of secret reports, we were required to attend a series of meetings where we listened to emissaries from the Pentagon who were experts at guarding secrets. These people displayed elaborate expensive charts and showed us films about German spies of World War II.

Perhaps because these security people sensed that Aberdeen was not fully impressed by their warnings of danger, they secretly arranged with a counter-intelligence unit to stage a full-scale test of our alertness. Under cover of an early-morning fog over Chesapeake Bay, four men boarded a motorboat a few miles below the proving ground. They were suited up in phony uniforms that vaguely resembled those worn by officers of the Red Army.

On schedule, the motorboat reached an area of sandy shoreline where the usual daily tests were beginning on tanks and other motorized vehicles. The four men in their Hollywood uniforms walked around for an hour or so snapping photographs of various secret machines. All during the war years, the ordnance people had grown accustomed to working while foreign officers from various friendly nations observed them, and so they paid little attention to these make-believe Russians. In fact, when the four men asked for a jeep to take them up to the headquarters area, the tank men readily supplied one.

On their way to the proving ground's headquarters, the phony Russians stopped off at the telephone exchange building, bound and gagged the two female employees, and then strode over to the headquarters building, demanding to see the commanding general. When they were admitted to the general's presence, they displayed their counter-intelligence badges, presented him with their rolls of exposed film, and informed him they had captured the proving ground.

The "Red Army" invasion created quite a commotion throughout the entire base. Within a few minutes after the "capture" of headquarters, the colonel to whom I was responsible burst breathlessly into my office to determine whether or not the TIB's security had been breached. At first he was vastly relieved to learn that the make-believe Russians had overlooked us, but then he became rather petulant because we had been ignored. After all, as he pointed out, it was comparable to a gang of robbers entering a bank and taking everything but the money. Aberdeen's payload of secrets was in our keeping, but the security testers had not even made an attempt to penetrate our defenses.

For the first time now a vague feeling of unease nudged at my consciousness. In my career I had occasionally been vexed by book thieves, who plague all librarians, but I had always thought of book thieves as selfish readers, or helpless kleptomaniacs, or people under some kind of pressures for information or relaxation. I had always held books in such high regard that I could not dislike people who liked them so well that they stole them. True, it was very annoying to lose a book by theft, but not disturbing enough to keep me awake nights. But now I began to lie sleepless into the small hours of the mornings, worrying about those hundreds of thousands of secret documents. Not one of those documents was aesthetically pleasing to the senses. Most of them were mimeographed, a hundred pages or so on cheap paper, stapled into repulsive cardboard covers of various depressing colors. They possessed none of the aromatic ink-and-paper smells of real books. They did not rest upright on shelves where readers might browse and choose; instead they lay locked in metal cabinets, retrievable only for the eyes of a few human beings who shared some part of the secrets revealed in their unlovely pages. All of them, the entire collection of hundreds of thousands, existed for one common purpose—the destruction of the enemy, whoever he might be, at some vague time in the future. They were not the sort of materials that librarians admire.

Shortly after the Red Army invasion, the commanding general who had been the principal victim was quietly transferred to some remote post in the hinterland, and a new general arrived, a lean-jawed veteran of the Pentagon foxholes. He was primed and ready to ferret out leaks in our security system. He knew very well where the secrets of Aberdeen lay, and one of his first acts was to visit the Technical Information Branch in company with the colonel to whom I reported. He made a thorough inspection of the old red brick structure where the library was housed, leading us around the building twice, his hawk's eyes studying its doors and windows. Then he led the way inside to consult our security procedures.

The procedures were complex enough; every civilian and military borrower of a secret document had to be cleared for various areas of research. A clearance meant that the FBI, the Army's own intelligence division, and God knows who else had looked into one's background from grandparents to birth—and then into one's schooling, drinking and sex habits, recreational interests, associates, reading matter, and private thoughts. A researcher cleared for automatic rifles might or might not be cleared for rockets, a tank man might be unable to see secrets on aerial guns, etc. A comparable campus situation would be a researcher into Chinese art not being permitted to borrow books on biology; or a chemistry professor not being able to borrow the novels of Henry James. One need not be a librarian to imagine the complicated records we had to keep on everybody who used the library.

At first, the general seemed satisfied with all this, but then he suddenly asked how long it had been since we had a showdown—that is, every secret document charged out brought in on short notice. I told him we had had no showdowns since I had been there, and none of my assistants, some of whom had been there through the war, could remember ever having a showdown. The general grew very excited about this, and the next day he issued an order that every one on the proving ground had to turn in his borrowed secret documents within twenty-four hours.

This order created about as much furor as the Red Army invasion. Offices and laboratories, desks and safes, were searched for every scrap of secret paper. By midafternoon of the day of judgment, our clerks were swamped and the entrance hallways filled with scientists and engineers carrying armloads of secret documents. In the midst of the confusion, the general appeared. He ordered me to keep going through the night if necessary. We worked until midnight, and surprisingly, only six documents were missing. Five were technical manuals in Japanese describing the operation of small arms that the Japanese Army used in the Pacific war. These manuals had been stamped SECRET at the time of their capture and had never been declassified. They were charged to a captain in the foreign weapons section. The sixth missing report was signed out to the proving ground's leading physicist, a man who had worn a colonel's uniform during the war but had recently become a civilian again. His name, let us say, was McCandlish.

At eight o'clock the next morning, the general gathered a board of inquiry around a long walnut table in his office. He had representatives from counter-intelligence, the security division, and the legal division, as well as my colonel and me to aid him in his inquisition of Dr. McCandlish and the captain from foreign weapons section.

The general first took up the matter of the five missing Japanese manuals. The captain charged with having them in his possession began his defense by claiming that the manuals should never have been marked SECRET, and even if they had been secret during the war, they were no longer so because the weapons they described could be found in dozens of museums across the country, and many of them were keepsakes of former soldiers who had brought them back from the Pacific.

The general would have none of that. A secret document, he declared, was a secret document until someone in authority declassified it. The captain replied that the manuals charged to him undoubtedly had been shipped along with the weapons they described to various museums. "All right," thundered the general, "you track them down, captain, and bring them back here."

Next it was Dr. McCandlish's turn. The general scolded him more gently than he had the captain, then tried to shame him by saying that a scientist of his great reputation should not have been so careless as to misplace a secret document. McCandlish was a thin-faced man with close-cropped hair graying at the temples. Quite calmly, he informed the general that he knew where the document was. He had taken it to a joint allied military conference in Paris some weeks before and had given it to a French physicist.

At this the general almost exploded. "You gave it to a Frenchman!" he shouted. "Don't you know the French are damned unreliable, probably have all sorts of secret agreements with the

Russians?"

McCandlish replied that he and the French scientist were working together on bomb-triggering devices and had exchanged information all through the war.

The general was shaking his head in dismay. "You'll have to get that document back, you know," he said hoarsely, "and I'll have to notify the Pentagon of your actions."

McCandlish remained calm. "There's no point in that," he replied. "I declassified the report this morning. It is no longer secret."

Someone at the table smothered a laugh, but the general's face reddened and we remained deadly quiet. The general then demanded to know by what authority McCandlish had declassified the report. The scientist replied offhandedly that he had written the report himself and therefore had the right to declassify it. He slipped a brown folder out of his briefcase and slid it across the table to the general. McCandlish said: "Here's the second copy." We could all see that the SECRET stamp on its face had been crossed out and initialed.

The general stared at the document for what seemed a long time; then he looked up, his face glowing with pleasure. "Very neatly done," he cried. "We're off the hook on that one. I'll report the five missing Japanese secret documents to the Pentagon to prove to them that we're on the qui vive here at Aberdeen, and it will also prove that our *own* secrets are safe. Right?"

Everyone was happy except the luckless captain from the foreign weapons section, and for a few days we had a period of euphoria in the TIB. The general even sent us a curt note in quadruplicate thanking us for our cooperation in the showdown. Then a few days later, he informed me through my colonel that a new surefire mechanical security alarm system would be installed immediately around the library building at a cost of several thousands of dollars.

The system consisted of strips of metallic tape fastened across all windows and the single entrance door. Whenever a window or door was opened a fraction of an inch, the tape connection was broken and a loud bell would be set to ringing not only outside the building, but in military police headquarters and also just above the desk of the officer-of-the-day in the administration building.

Only my chief assistant and I were authorized to carry keys to the alarm system. Each evening when we locked up, the system had to be activated with a turn of the key, and each morning it had to be neutralized. For several days after it was installed, I went home each evening convinced that the new alarm system would keep my hundreds of thousands of secrets quite safe until I returned the next morning. Then one night, an artillery research team set up an after-dark operation. At the first boom of a big gun, every window on the library building reverberated, breaking the tape connections momentarily and setting all the alarm bells to ringing.

I heard about it from the officer-of-the-day, who telephoned me at home: "Get out here," he shouted. "Your security's been breached!"

By the time I reached the building, the military police had several cars drawn up around it and searchlights were blazing against each wall. They had even brought in a throbbing fire engine just in case it was needed. The officer-of-the-day and a military police officer were pacing up and down at the base of the entrance steps, the big alarm bell jangling above them. I turned it off with my magic key and we made a thorough search of the building but of course found nothing. I locked the door and reactivated the alarm, but before we had gotten back to our cars one of the big guns boomed again and the bell responded like an answering echo.

We all knew immediately that the big guns had set off the alarm, and we also knew that as long as the guns continued firing they would keep setting off the alarm if we turned it on again. The officer-of-the-day and the military police officer asked me what they should do. I suggested they call the general and ask his advice. They were reluctant until I pointed out that it was the general who had installed the system.

They called the general, and his solution was simple. Shut off the alarm and assign a detail of military police to guard the library building until it was opened for business the following morning. Next day the general issued an order requiring that I, the chief of the Technical Information Branch, be notified twenty-four hours in advance of any artillery firing at night. On those nights an eight-man police guard would report to me at the closing hour to take over the duties of the automatic alarm system. This procedure placed another layer of paperwork on my already burdened desk, but at least no more summoning telephone calls interrupted my sleep. That is, not until the night of the big blizzard.

It was one of those sudden snowstorms that sweep up the East Coast, and sometime around midnight the rising wind rattled the windows of the library hard enough to set off the bells. The officer-of-the-day soon had me out of bed. It was not easy getting to the proving ground through fierce snow-laden winds over four miles of icy road. The old library building behind its curtain of swirling snowflakes and illuminated by searchlights reminded me of a Grandma Moses Christmas card.

I rushed up the steps and shut off the clamorous bell. But a few seconds after I had reactivated it, the howling wind set off the alarm again.

The military police officer growled at me: "What the hell do we do now?"

I turned it off again and made a suggestion. "Let's all go back to our warm places," I said, "and forget about this storm-tossed building. Not even a Cossack Russian would come out to steal secrets on a night like this."

The military police officer rejected my suggestion. It was all right for a civilian like me to take a chance like that, but *he* would be risking his neck. He assigned a guard and I went back home to my warm bed. But I could not sleep for thinking of those eight miserable military police who had been detailed to guard the library. In a series of disturbing dreams I could see them marching around and around that windswept structure, frost forming on eyelids and nostrils, their uniforms ripped ragged under icy blasts of the blizzard, marching and marching until the soles of their boots wore through, marching until their feet began bleeding to leave a trail of frozen blood on the beaten snow. In my dreams they were noble patriots all, guarding the secrets of the nation in the same spirit that George Washington's men prevailed at Valley Forge.

Involved as I had become with that delicate alarm system, the paperwork connected with it, and the growing amount of other military and civil service red tape, I had very few moments left over in each day to give much thought to any contrived raids against my security defenses. Consequently I was not on the qui vive one morning when a jaunty young lieutenant came in and wanted to be escorted into a vault to select a batch of secret photographs needed for a hurry-up conference. Recoilless rifles was what he wanted, and a check of our records showed that he was cleared for recoilless rifles. I took him into the vault and stood guarding him while he searched the photo file. A confederate, as he turned out to be later, called me suddenly from the door of the vault. He had a secret document that he wished to leave in my keeping. I carelessly turned my back on the lieutenant, walked to the vault door, took the offered document, and signed a receipt for it. When I turned back to the lieutenant, he said he had the secret recoilless rifle photographs he wanted. I made him sign for them and cheerfully sent him on his way.

Ten minutes later my telephone rang. I recognized the general's voice immediately. He ordered me to report to his office right away. Something was wrong, I knew that; and I wasn't too surprised when I walked into his office and saw that he had assembled his court of inquisitors around the shiny walnut table. In the middle of the table was a photograph of a rocket device with SECRET stamped across it in big purple letters.

I stared at the photograph for a moment, then looked at the faces around the table. The jaunty lieutenant and his confederate wore smirks on their faces that combined condescension with triumph. Nor did I find any sympathy in the faces of the security men, and then I was surprised to see Dr. McCandlish sitting there, too. He winked at me just as the general thundered out a denunciation of my carelessness. All those drills and lectures on security had been wasted on me, he charged. He pointed at the photograph on the table and shouted: "That is a secret rocket!" He then asked dramatically: "Is the lieutenant cleared for rockets? Do you know?"

"He is not," I replied. At this the general accused me of being doubly guilty.

Dr. McCandlish finally spoke up: "That rocket's a pretty hot item," he said. "I should have classified it *top* secret except that I feared such a high classification might hinder its rapid development."

"Good God," the general said. "Top secret!" He glowered at me and said he would have to report my negligence to the Pentagon immediately.

Dr. McCandlish interrupted again. "But general," he said. "Mr. Brown is *not* the guilty party. The *lieutenant* stole the photograph with the aid of an accomplice. Neither man is cleared for rockets, and if you report this incident to the Pentagon you're going to have a hell of a lot of explaining to do about that. Only three men at this table are cleared to see that photograph lying there—you, me, and Mr. Brown."

The general's face turned brick-red; he pointed a finger at the photograph and ordered the lieutenant: "Turn that damn thing over." The lieutenant did so with trembling fingers; the smirk had vanished from his face.

And then the general groaned: "But I'm under orders to report security failures to Washington. And this was a security failure."

McCandlish came to his rescue. He said, "But this was not a *real* failure, general. It was only a *simulated* failure."

The general's eyes brightened. "Simulated. Yes, of course," he cried. "By God, McCandlish, you saw through my little test, didn't you? I only wanted to keep those people over at the TIB on the qui vive." He rose from his chair, lifted the secret photograph from the table, and handed it to me, ordering me to return it to the vault. He turned then and shook his finger at the most junior officer in the room, the no-longer swaggering lieutenant. "You'd better watch your step, lieutenant," the general growled. "You could get court-martialed for what you did today."

It was on a Saturday that I finally came to a parting of the ways with the Cold War at Aberdeen. I was home, in the front yard, puttering around in a flower bed when a long black Lincoln sedan rolled up at the curb. A tall man wearing a gray suit and a wide-brimmed gray hat leaped out and came striding across the lawn. For a second or two he stood studying my grimy hands, my ragged workshirt, muddy shoes, and unshaven Saturday face. He said suspiciously: "You're not the Chief of Technical Information Branch, surely?"

I had to admit that I was. He pulled out a leather card case and flashed it in my face. "Counter-Intelligence Division," he said in a voice like Humphrey Bogart's. "It's an emergency. You have a microfilm reader in your library, don't you?"

I told him we did have a microfilm reader, and he said he wanted to use it right away. Emergency. As quickly as I could, I washed up and changed clothes. As I hurried out the front door, Sally asked, "What do they want?"

"I don't know," I shouted back. "Something about microfilm."

Before I reached the black car, the man in gray swung the rear door open for me, and we roared away. The man who was driving glanced back at me; he also wore gray and had a broad face somewhat like a frog's.

When we reached the entrance to the proving ground, we had to show our identity cards, and I noted that the military policeman seemed to linger a while over those of the counter-intelligence men. I began to grow suspicious. Maybe they were not *genuine* C.I.D. men. No matter who they might be, if I let them in the library building, they could easily overpower me, bind me up, and ransack the secret files. They were clever to choose a Saturday, a day when no one else would be around. What the hell was I going to do?

As the car rolled up to the old brick structure of the TIB that housed all the secrets of Aberdeen, I said boldly, "Drive on over to headquarters." I had placed one hand instinctively on the door latch, intending to leap out if they pulled guns on me. Both men whirled to face me, objecting strenuously that this would only kill more time.

"It's standard operating procedure," I lied. The driver swore, and meshed the gears into a quick leap forward. He drove over to headquarters and parked, and I led them in to see the officer-of-the-day. He was a captain I had seen around, but I did not know his name. He was half asleep, but he jumped up and swept an empty beer bottle off his desk, obviously annoyed because we were there on a Saturday morning.

The two C.I.D. men were even *more* annoyed as they explained what they wanted. The officer-of-the-day glanced at me and wanted to know what was the problem. Couldn't I let them use the reading machine?

I told him that I would let them in the TIB building if *he* would give me a signed order to do so. The officer-of-the-day shook his head uncertainly; the C.I.D. men grew angrier and angrier. At last the tall C.I.D. man demanded to talk to the officer-of-the-day's commander. That was the general, of course, who usually played golf on Saturdays, but for some reason he was at home that morning.

As the tall C.I.D. man told his story to the general over the telephone, he tried to keep his grating Humphrey Bogart voice a bit less peremptory than when he had addressed the captain and me. When he finished, I could hear the sound of the general on the phone. He wanted to talk to me. I took the phone. The general's voice was loaded with caution and distrust. He asked, "How does it look to you?"

I answered, "It could be OK and again it might not be."

I could hear the general breathing heavily. He said, "Coming here on a Saturday looks mighty suspicious to me. Whatever you do, don't let them get any closer to the Technical Information Branch than they are right now. Put the officer-of-the-day back on."

Taking the phone, the officer muttered a few "yes, sirs," and "no, sirs," then suddenly turned to me and asked, "How heavy is a microfilm reader?"

I told him the one we had probably weighed a hundred pounds. "Could two men carry it?"

I told him yes.

The general's solution was to get a truck from the motor pool, two prisoners and a guard from the stockade, the prisoners to do the lifting of the microfilm reader in and out of the truck and transferring it over to the headquarters building. It took an hour or so to get all this done. Alongside the officer-of-the-day's desk I found an electric outlet, plugged the microfilm reader in, and turned on the light. Both C.I.D. men were hovering over me. The tall one said they wanted to look at the microfilm privately but that they didn't know how to operate the machine. I showed them how to feed the film and adjust the focus, and then moved away. After a while they called me over to take a look at what was on the viewing screen. The frog-faced

C.I.D. man asked excitedly, "That's Russian stuff, isn't it?" It was clearly a reproduction of a page of print in Russian.

In whispers, they then told me they would have to take me into their confidence. It seemed they had one of the civilian scientists from the proving ground under surveillance. They would not tell me his name, but early that morning after the man left his apartment they had entered and searched the place until they found the microfilm in a dresser drawer. The man was a young mathematical scientist, they said, and he had been under suspicion ever since he was spotted attending a Pete Seeger folksong and political rally in Baltimore. What they wanted me to tell them was why the film had the name of the proving ground library on the first frame. Was it *secret?* When I told them, no, it was not secret, they seemed terribly disappointed.

Well, then, they asked, might the young scientist have stolen it from us?

I told them there would have been no reason for him to steal it; we probably had ordered it for him.

They asked: Why would anybody at Aberdeen want a Russian film?

I replied that this film was an article from a Soviet periodical, evidently a ballistics journal.

Can *you* read Russian? they asked with growing suspicion.

I said no, but that I had learned the alphabet and a few key words so that I could recognize the titles of periodicals.

Well, where had this microfilm come from? they asked. I rolled the microfilm to the end where there was a photocopy of our order sheet and told them we had ordered it from Harvard University.

"*Harvard,*" the frog-faced man said. "That place is full of Red professors, all right." But he seemed disappointed somehow.

The tall man asked hopefully, "Can you find out the name of the person who actually ordered this microfilm?" I pointed to the bottom of the order sheet on the screen, at a name typed in by our order clerk. He stared at the name and then whispered to me: "Erase that name from your memory forever."

I said I would try. But I never did. I knew that brilliant young mathematician well. I knew he had not the slightest interest in politics, but he was slightly mad about folksongs, especially those of Pete Seeger.

In those days it was not easy to find library jobs, but I found another one, much to the displeasure of the colonel to whom I reported. It was not that the colonel admired my abilities or was especially fond of me or anything like that. As he put it in his honest, direct, military way, he just hated the thought of having to break in a new chief for the TIB.

He said with some puzzlement: "I thought you were happy here."

I replied that I had grown weary of being a Cold Warrior.

"Oh, that," he said. "The Cold War is only a game. It keeps congressional appropriations fat for us every year."

I had been there long enough to have noticed that great crises always broke out in sensitive areas around the world whenever Congress was debating military appropriations. But I had never thought of the Cold War as being a game.

I had believed it was real.

The colonel continued to probe. "If it's more money you want," he said, "I'm sure we can do something about that."

I did not tell him that I was taking a sizable cut in salary to go to the new job.

"Come on," the colonel said brightly. "Name your price."

I named it. "I'll work for you one more year," I said. "For a million dollars. In advance."

CHAPTER TWELVE

Hafiz and the English Lord

FROM ABERDEEN I WENT TO the University of Illinois at Urbana to become the Librarian of the College of Agriculture. Illinois is one of the great agricultural states, and the college and its library reflect this splendid circumstance. Within a few weeks I renewed my old familiarity with the literature of the subjects I had delighted in while I was at the Beltsville Research Center—-livestock, plants, soils, trees, farm machinery, markets, and rural life—the literature of the science and art of farming. During these first postwar years, returning veterans of World War II doubled and tripled the enrollments and there was much work for librarians to do, especially with graduate students who were rusty from years of absence from classrooms.

In the atmosphere of a university campus there is something that lures writers to write, and I was soon engaged in long-distance collaboration with Martin Schmitt on the two photographic histories that followed the one on American Indians. Salaries were low for librarians in those pre-Sputnik years, and my income was insufficient for repairing or replacing automobiles, taking family vacations, paying for mortgages, and so on. To supplement my income I wrote several formula Western novels, all based on actual incidents in the West. In the midst of this pleasant and slightly profitable avocation I stumbled upon the unpublished letters of two brothers who had served in the Union Army during the Civil War. They had accompanied Colonel Benjamin Grierson on a cavalry raid through Mississippi at the time General Grant was attempting to cross the Mississippi River and capture Vicksburg. Only bits and pieces of this dramatic adventure had been published, and so I resolved to write the complete history of Grierson's Raid.

As Grierson's personal and official papers were in the Illinois

State Library at Springfield, I was obliged to take an occasional day's leave to travel there for research. On the occasion of one of these journeys to Springfield, I became acquainted with an unusual graduate student in my college, and in the months that followed I was an attentive witness to his remarkable odyssey in learning.

The first time I saw Hamid Hafiz was soon after he arrived at the University of Illinois and came into the agriculture library. He was moving cautiously into the library stacks, his hesitant footsteps and his face revealing amazement rather than anxiety. His large liquid eyes were like those of a child who has been allowed to wander alone into the edge of a forest. There was something so incongruous about him that I could not help but stare, but I do not suppose he was aware of my presence at all. He was too absorbed in the books, his eyes following the rows and rows of them with disbelief as though suspecting the apparent endlessness of shelves to be an optical illusion created by some trick of opposite mirrors.

He was wearing a black achkan—a close-fitting, high-necked coat that flared below the waist and reached to the knees of his tight gray Oriental trousers. His white shirt was buttoned at the collar. There was an air of Rudyard Kipling about him. The Khyber Pass, Kabul, and Peshawar flashed into my mind. I thought he might be one of the new students from India; we always had several arrivals each autumn on an exchange program. But he was not. He was a Pakistani, and he had come to America all alone, friendless, almost penniless.

As I learned afterward, he had applied for and won a scholarship that paid for his tuition, and the university had placed him in a house with other foreign students. After a few days he must have become aware of the attention his outlandish garb was creating. He showed up in the library one chilly morning wearing a gray sweatshirt and a pair of cheap brown corduroys. He wore this costume through the winter. I never suspected until later that these were the only American clothes he could afford. They were always clean; he must have washed them out at night two or three times a week. He never wore the achkan again, even in the coldest weather.

I did not learn his name until one of his instructors sent him to see me about a research project he was beginning. "I am Hamid Ali

Hafiz," he said politely in rich British English. It was the first time I had heard him speak, and I thought of Kipling again. He seemed in awe, not of me but of the position I held—librarian in charge of all those endless shelves of books. To me it was a refreshing attitude, and I had no difficulty liking Hamid Hafiz.

For the next week or so he visited my office almost every day to discuss some point or other about the literature of his research. I discovered that he was borrowing at least a dozen volumes each evening, taking them to his room to read, and then returning them the next day to choose another dozen.

One day I remarked: "You must read very fast."

"I had very good British teachers," he replied proudly.

He seemed reluctant to tell me more about himself. I guessed that he must be experiencing the homesickness that attacks foreign students about the middle of their first semester. I knew he was lonely, being the only Pakistani in the college, but I did not know how lonely until one day he told me matter-of-factly: "I am, sir, of the lowest caste in my country."

I laughed, thinking he was joking, and I said something about the caste system belonging to the past and surely it could not be a part of modern Pakistan. "The caste system cannot be changed," he said seriously, and went on: "In my lifetime I can rise only to the next caste above. I hope that by earning a degree from an American university I can marry above my caste and then my children will be of that caste."

By the end of the first semester, Hafiz's carefully hoarded personal funds were almost depleted. After making a few inquiries, he discovered that the only employment available to foreigners were student jobs within the university. Looking over the lists, he noted that library assistantships were open for students. He immediately came to see me.

I knew that two or three student library assistants would be dropping out at the end of the semester, but I was hesitant to employ him at first because in the past we had found that foreign students who had no library training were not very useful to us. They had language difficulties in dealing with other students; they did not comprehend the catalog and classification system and were slow in locating or shelving books. I balanced my hesitancy with the awareness that Hafiz had already read several hundred books in the library and I suspected that he knew exactly where every volume was shelved.

I said then: "Student assistants are required to have a B average."

He replied, "My grades are all A's. You may inquire of this to the Dean of Students."

Without further ado I told him that he could have the job, and during the three years he worked there I never regretted the decision. He was a natural librarian.

During the early spring I discovered in casual conversation that although Hafiz had been in the United States more than six months, all that he had seen of America was an airport in Chicago and the combined towns of Champaign–Urbana. He said to me: "Before I return to Pakistan, I have a great desire to visit the home of Abraham Lincoln in Springfield. While a schoolboy I read everything I could about him because he reminded me of myself. He was very poor, but in order to rise above his background he read everything he could find to read."

"He was of the lowest caste," I said, "but he became President of the United States."

Hafiz shook his head and declared solemnly, "He must have had the blood of an English lord in his veins."

"Why do you say this?" I asked.

He replied, "People of low-caste blood could not rise like he did."

"You're doing it," I said.

He turned his head so that his slightly hooked nose was in profile, and closed one eye. "I have long suspected," he said, "that I am the bastard son of an English lord."

Two or three weeks after this conversation I reached a point in my research for Grierson's Raid that required me to travel to Springfield to use the State Historical Library. As I would be spending the day in Lincoln country, I asked Hafiz if he would like to go along and visit the Lincoln shrines while I was doing my research. He accepted immediately and like a good scholar hurried off to make arrangements to be absent from scheduled classes.

When I picked him up early the next morning, Hafiz was wearing a neat gray suit and a bright orange necktie, an ensemble that he had recently acquired with his earnings. We were quickly out into flat farming country under a clean blue sky. The Illinois prairies have always reminded me of the open sea, and after springtime rains the land resembles dark rolling ocean waves with shoots of corn and soybeans streaked like green foam across their wet blackness. We sped along the smooth two-lane highway, Hafiz viewing the vast expanse with wonder.

"Where are the people?" he asked.

I pointed to the distant farmhouses with their accompanying barns that were scattered around the miles of level prairie. "Likely they're at home watching television or reading the city papers. Or perhaps they've driven into town. The crops are all planted, and if they have livestock they've been fed for the day, probably by automated feeders and waterers."

He said: "If we were in my country, this road—and it would be only a third as wide as this road—would be so filled with people and animals you would have to drive slower than you could walk. You would be sounding your horn every minute, and sheep and cattle would lie down in front of your wheels. I would get out and walk ahead of you with a big stick so as to make a pathway for your automobile."

Every ten minutes or so we would pass the edge of a small village—church, school, small store, filling station, grain elevators—and rarely did we see more than two or three people. Only through the eyes of Hafiz did I come to realize how big and empty the Midwestern farm country really is. To him it was almost frightening.

I turned on the radio to get the morning news. The newscaster was talking about the sighting of a flying saucer in Texas. When he finished I asked Hafiz what he thought of flying saucers.

"How long have you been seeing them in America?" he asked.

"Since World War II," I said. "Every year or so there is an epidemic of flying saucers in the sky."

"In Pakistan we have been seeing such things for thousands of years. To a Bhag-Nari nomad, seeing a strange object in the sky is no more unusual than sighting a bird." I glanced at him, at that roguish profile with the slightly hooked nose. Was this the profile of an English lord? Suspecting he was putting me on in some sly Oriental way, I turned off the radio and we talked about Abraham Lincoln for a few minutes.

And then he began telling me about how he was the first member of his nomadic tribe to learn to read and write and how he managed to find his way to the United States of America.

When he was very young his Bhag-Nari tribesmen moved constantly from place to place, seeking pasturage for their livestock, collecting whatever nature provided for their existence. Before he was six, Hafiz was given a camel to care for, and he probably would have been an untutored wanderer to this day had not his tribe chanced to camp near a town where there was a British school. The efficient pedagogues in charge took seriously the official decree that all children upon reaching the age of six must enter school, at the expense of the state if necessary. The Britishers paid a visit to the nomads' camp, hauled in young Hamid Hafiz over the protests of his indignant father and uncles, and clapped him into the boarding school.

A few nights later, moving with all the stealth and cunning of practiced thieves, Hafiz's male relatives invaded the school's dormitory and recovered the unhappy prisoner. For a day or two he was back with his camel in the free nomadic world, but the British authorities caught up with the tribe and reincarcerated the boy. After waiting a reasonable length of time, Hafiz's relatives repeated the raid, but once again the stubborn authorities pursued and claimed back the freed young student. Several weeks elapsed before the undaunted Bhag-Naris came back for a third try, but this time Hafiz refused to go with them. He had grown to like the regular meals, the warm beds, and most of all the mysteries of printed words, the roomful of books filled with pictures and symbols of a strange world that lay outside the world he knew.

For refusing to go with his father and uncles, Hamid Hafiz was rejected by the tribe, and he did not see them again for a very long time. During this period of his life, Pakistan and India became separate independent nations, and there was much turmoil and bloodshed along the borders. Like the other young students, Hafiz learned to fear the approach of enemies but luckily escaped the bloody massacres. He buried himself in his studies and became the star pupil in the school. He also read every volume in the small library. His teachers then lent him their personal books, and when he graduated they arranged for him to attend a small agricultural college in a nearby city. By this time Hafiz's kinsmen had accepted the fact that he was a young man of importance, and they invited him to return to the tribe. He joined them for a few days, astounding them with his ability to read and write and frightening them with his knowledge of the great world. His father took a fierce pride in his wayward son, but his mother was sure that devils had taken him from her and she wept when he told her he was going back to school.

In the agricultural college, Hafiz was bored by all the courses except economics, but he was so brilliant in that subject that in his second year he was put to work tutoring other students. After his senior year he became an instructor in agricultural economics. In the meantime, his British friends and mentors had been leaving one by one as Pakistanis moved into key positions in their new country. For the first time in his life, Hafiz became painfully aware of his low caste and fell to worrying about his future. He lived penuriously, saving as many rupees as possible until at last he was able to buy an acre of land. This gave him a certain sense of security, as well as a feeling of pride because not only was he the first member of his tribe to learn to read and write, he was also the first to own land. Yet he knew from the attitude of his colleagues that he was boxed in because of his low caste. No matter how hard he worked or studied, he would never be considered a genuine scholar, never advance in his profession, *unless he obtained a degree from a British or an American university*. To accomplish this would require a fortune greater than any amount he could save in a lifetime. He was trapped. But then one day he opened an economics journal from America and read therein an announcement of scholarships in the United States open to Asian students. He applied immediately and several months later was notified that he had been selected and should report to the University of Illinois for classes at the beginning of the next semester.

In a glow of euphoria, he announced his good fortune to everyone and set about preparing for his journey to America. He quickly came up against a hard fact: his total savings was not half enough to pay his airfare. After a day or so of mental turmoil, he reluctantly decided that he must sell his acre of land. By this time everybody in the community had heard that Hafiz needed money to go to America, and when he went to the land dealers, they offered him only half what he had paid for his acre. He could find no one who would offer more than that amount; the price had been fixed by his urgency.

In desperation he went to the director of the college, a Pakistani who had recently replaced a departing British educator. Hafiz explained to him: "I need the full value of my acre of land to pay my way to America."

"I do not need any land," the director replied.

"I will buy it back from you with interest after I return with my American degree," Hafiz promised.

"Why should *you* be going to America?" the director complained. "If anyone from this school should be going to America, I should be the one. Not a low-caste nomad who believes himself to be a scholar. No, I do not wish to buy your land at any price, Hamid Hafiz."

In very low spirits, Hafiz returned to his daily routine. He was trapped again, his beautiful dream floating further away with every passing hour. One night while rolling sleepless on his bed, he decided that he must use some of his savings to travel to the capital where he would try to obtain an audience with the American ambassador. Perhaps the Americans would lend him the money he needed. At least it was worth trying.

He never saw the ambassador. The first embassy clerk he encountered ruffled through the papers from the University of Illinois and inquired with bored politeness: "What's your problem, Mr. Hafiz?"

"Sir, I have not enough money to travel to America."

"Oh? Didn't they inform you of the Fulbright program?"

Hafiz had never heard of the Fulbright program.

"All foreigners receiving scholarships from the United States are entitled to travel funds," the official explained, reaching for a form. "Just fill that out, Mr. Hafiz, and we'll make the arrangements."

And so, a few weeks later, dressed in his new black achkan, which he had purchased to lend dignity to his person, Hafiz arrived in Urbana, Illinois.

Some months later, here he was, riding with me into Springfield to pay his respects to Abraham Lincoln. We drove past the cemetery where the martyred president lies buried, and I told him of the attempt made long ago by a gang of Chicago criminals to steal Lincoln's body and hold it for ransom. He shook his head despairingly: "And I thought my Bhag-Naris were the world's greatest thieves."

We found a parking place near the building where I was to seek materials about General Benjamin Grierson and his raid into Mississippi. Hafiz went in with me so that he would know where to find me after he had finished his morning sightseeing. Our arrangement was that he would visit the adjoining museum and Lincoln's house and then meet me for lunch. I would then drive him out to the cemetery where he said he would spend some time in meditation and then walk back into town. It would be a rather long walk, but he thought it would be a good way to see the place where Lincoln had lived.

He went off, waving his tourist's map cheerily, leaving me alone with my notebooks. The morning sped away, and when I glanced up at the wall clock the hands were pointing toward noon. I began arranging my papers in expectation of Hafiz's return. A few minutes later a clerk from the entrance desk brought me a folded note. She whispered, "Someone from the secretary's office just brought this over for you."

"Whose secretary?" I asked.

"The Secretary of State," she explained. "Mr. Paul Powell."

I unfolded the note. The heading was in big boldface type: MEMO FROM THE DESK OF PAUL POWELL, SECRETARY OF STATE. Beneath was Hafiz's schoolboy scrawl:

Will be unable to join you for lunch, regretfully. Am being conducted on honorary Lincoln tour for foreign visitors. Shall I see you at four o'clock?—*Hamid Hafiz*

Hafiz told me about his adventures after he returned late in the afternoon and we were started back to Urbana.

"When I left you this morning," he said, "I walked over to the other building and entered a corridor where there were many photographs of the same man. His gray hair was nicely combed and he was smiling out of all the pictures. As I walked along, the photographs grew larger until I came to one that filled the side of a wall. 'Who is this man?' I asked myself. 'He must be the greatest man in all Illinois.'

"I walked through a door beside the gigantic picture, and a handsome young woman at a desk asked me to sign my name in a registry book. I did so, and in the place for home address I put down my college in Pakistan. The handsome young woman smiled at me and told me to take a seat. I supposed I was waiting for a guide to come and show me through the museum. The young woman went away somewhere with the registry book and then returned to her desk. After a few more minutes there was a buzzing sound on the desk. She said to me: 'The secretary will see you now.' I did not know who the secretary was, but I followed her to a big door, and when she opened it I went inside and there sitting at an immense desk was this man with the nicely combed gray hair, the one whose photographs were everywhere and who I had decided must be the greatest man in Illinois.

"I assure you that I was so overcome with emotion that I could not speak. I was trying to tell him that there had been some terrible mistake, that I, Hamid Hafiz, a low-caste nomad from Pakistan had no excuse for being in the presence of the greatest man in Illinois.

"But he smiled at me, just as he did out of the big photographs and said: 'Welcome to Springfield, Mr. Hafiz. I'm Paul Powell, Secretary of State.' He came around from behind his desk and shook my hand. I was so agitated that I became like a child again. He motioned me to sit on a big leather divan and then he sat down beside me, still smiling. 'We get visitors here from all over the world,' he said to me. 'They come to pay homage to Abraham Lincoln. From all over. But I don't recollect any from Pakistan. Not since I have been in this office. You're our first from Pakistan. Did you fly in?'"

Hafiz was not especially good at imitating American accents, but he seemed to have total recall and a good ear for speech patterns. Even through his British English I could hear the southern Illinois drawl of Paul Powell.

"I told Secretary Powell I had come by automobile from Urbana," Hafiz continued, "and he said: 'Oh, I reckon you been visiting our great university. What you think of our great state, Mr. Hafiz?' I was about to tell him I was only a mere student at the university, but he interrupted me: 'Could I offer you a drink, Mr. Hafiz?' 'A glass of water, sir,' I said, and he laughed and slapped his leg. 'I always take a sip of bourbon to get the day started, Mr. Hafiz. You ought to try it.'

"He poured some water out of a fancy decanter into a paper cup and handed it to me. I was much mortified that so great a man should be waiting upon me, Hamid Hafiz. He then poured himself some liquor into another cup, lifted it up, and said with a big smile: 'Well, here's to Pakistan.' 'Thank you, sir,' I said, and then there was a knock on the door, and the handsome young woman announced: 'The photographers are here, Mr. Secretary.'

"Two young men came in, one carrying a big folding camera, the other a small camera. They told me to stand up beside the secretary. The secretary said: 'Now get us between the flags.' We stood shoulder to shoulder between two flags, one of the United States, the other of the State of Illinois. Naturally I was becoming more and more nervous about all this. My palms were wet and my heart was pounding. But the secretary kept talking and talking, pausing now and then to take a sip from his cup.

"When the photographers finished their work and started to go, the Secretary turned to me and asked: 'How long you plan to stay with us, Mr. Hafiz?' I told him I must leave at four o'clock, and he said to the photographers: 'You boys have some good prints ready for Mr. Hafiz by four, now, hear me, and don't forget I want to approve the one you send out to the press services. That picture you sent out of me and the big man from Tunisia last week, it didn't help the old image, you know what I mean.'"

By the time Hafiz reached this point in his narration, we were out of Springfield and on the main highway. Hafiz was shaking his head, still finding it difficult to believe the things that had happened to him that day. He had a collection of booklets, folders, and brown envelopes in his lap, and from out of the envelopes he took several enlarged photographs and stared at them. He asked: "Why would the secretary wish to be photographed with me?" I glanced at the top photograph, Hafiz looking very dignified, Powell posing with his politician's smile.

I said, "He likes to get his picture in the newspapers. You being in the photograph, a visitor from a faraway country paying a pilgrimage to Lincoln land, makes it news. A lot of papers will use the photograph, but they'd never print a picture of Paul Powell just standing there alone in his office? You understand?"

Hafiz was still puzzled. "But is he not the boss of Illinois? Why does he not simply tell the newspapers when he wishes his photograph to be printed?"

"Oh, no. He has great political power, but he is not the boss of the newspapers."

Hafiz held one of the photographs, letting the late afternoon sunlight illuminate it. "In this one," he asked, "do you not think I have the look of an English lord?"

"No," I said. "You look like a Bhag-Nari camel driver who has shaved off his beard, taken a bath, and dressed himself in an English lord's clothing."

"A Bhag-Nari camel driver could never be photographed with the Secretary of State of Illinois. That I know." His voice was serious, but he smiled mysteriously. "My father is a Muslim and had more than one wife, don't you know. I am not entirely certain if my mother is truly my mother. Or if the man I know as my father is truly my father."

During the remainder of the journey home, he told me of how he had been taken on a morning tour of Springfield in a big limousine driven by a friendly black man. They had visited the Lincoln home and tomb and then returned for a luncheon with Secretary Powell and several men and women from Chicago. Hafiz said he was introduced to all the guests, but he was relieved that during the luncheon they paid very little attention to him but talked incessantly among themselves of politics, contracts, money, and automobile licenses.

I explained that one of Paul Powell's duties was the collection of millions of dollars in fees from automobile drivers and owners. "He is also the official state librarian," I said, "but he only visits the library to have his picture made on special occasions."

"The secretary is a most extraordinary man," Hafiz remarked. "He never gave me an opportunity to explain that I am only a poor student. This afternoon while the friendly black man was showing me the restored village of New Salem where Abraham Lincoln lived as a young man, I told him that I was only a student at the University of Illinois. He laughed very hard and then said it wouldn't make any difference to Mr. Paul Powell because he was a real democratic man."

(Some years afterward when Powell died suddenly, an unexplained hoard of shoe boxes filled with more than a million dollars was found in his living quarters. I was on the point of sending the news clippings to Hamid Hafiz, but by this time Hafiz himself had become an important official in Pakistan, and I did not wish to add to his disillusionment with American politics.)

At the end of his second semester at the university, Hafiz received a master's degree, and his abilities so impressed his professors that he was awarded a scholarship to enter the Ph.D. program. He continued to work a few hours each week in the library to keep himself in pocket money.

His confidence in himself increased gradually, and I never heard him mention the caste system again until one day early in the autumn he asked me if I had met Saleem Aziz. "He has just come from my country," he explained.

I replied that I had not met Saleem, but that I was glad Hafiz now had a compatriot to talk with.

"He will have little to do with me," Hafiz said. "Saleem is of a high caste and his father is very rich." He went on to tell me that Saleem's father had come over with his son from Pakistan and had attempted to purchase the young man's admittance to Harvard and some other Ivy League universities. On discovering that this was not possible, the wealthy father had accepted the advice of one of the registrars and settled for a Big Ten university. The father chose Illinois because it was in the heart of America's rich farming country and he wanted his son to manage his lands after returning to Pakistan. And so Saleem Aziz, who had come to America to obtain a Harvard degree, ended up in the College of Agriculture at the University of Illinois.

Before a month was out, the rich Pakistani's son became an incubus to Hafiz. He flaunted his money and position over the former nomad, yet was constantly beseeching Hafiz to write papers for him, even to attend classes as his surrogate. Hafiz patiently explained that such practices were frowned upon in America, and he angered Saleem by turning down all his offers of money. Hafiz refused to share an apartment with Saleem even though the wealthy young man offered to pay all expenses. "He would make a servant of me," Hafiz declared. "Besides, he has become a companion of gangsters and fast girls from Chicago and spends too much time with them. He drinks strong liquors constantly and is no longer a good Muslim. I have warned him that he must attend classes and take all the examinations but he only laughs at me. He says his father will pay for all those things."

In a bold attempt to regain favor with his instructors and attract attention to himself, Saleem arranged through the influence of his father for the Pakistani ambassador to come from Washington and address the faculty and students. For a few days Saleem was much in evidence, conferring with the deans, posting and passing out leaflets, and giving interviews to the press and television. He even made a personal call on the university president to invite him to the ceremonies.

Saleem also arranged for the dean of the college and himself to meet the ambassador at the airport shortly before noon on the following Monday. They were to drive the ambassador to a special luncheon for a few exclusive guests, and in the afternoon, accompanied by Saleem, he would drop in on two or three seminars and then deliver his lecture in the main auditorium. Saleem, of course, would introduce him with a little speech which he had persuaded

Hafiz to write for him. Hafiz had secretly shown it to me, asking for comments. Like everything else that Hafiz set his mind to, the introduction was perfect.

On Monday morning at ten, Hafiz reported with his usual punctuality for the two hours he was scheduled to work at the library circulation desk. He was dressed in his best suit and bright orange necktie, but there was such a brooding air about him that I asked if he felt unwell. "Oh, no," he replied. "I worry about Saleem. He went to Chicago with his gangster friends and has not returned."

"He'll be back on time," I said. "He has too much at stake in this visit of the ambassador."

"You do not know Saleem. He thinks he can drink as much liquor as the Chicagoans, but he has not their immunity. He becomes a wild man."

At eleven o'clock a telephone call came for Hafiz from the dean's office. He talked very softly into the phone, hung up, and dialed a number. There was no answer. He came to my desk and said apologetically: "It is necessary that I leave now."

"That's all right," I told him, "Mrs. Alleman can fill in for you."

He remained standing in front of my desk, his eyes almost beseeching when I glanced up. "I was hoping that you would forbid me to leave," he said. "The dean wishes me to take Saleem's place when we meet the ambassador. I do not think I can do this."

"Why not?"

"The ambassador will be insulted if he is met by a low-caste countryman."

"If you don't tell him, how the hell will he know what caste you are?"

"He will know." Hafiz sighed. "I know he will know."

And so the low-caste son of a Bhag-Nari nomad received the ambassador of his country in America, dined with him, accompanied him on a tour of the campus, and then introduced him with such a brilliant little speech that afterward the ambassador made a point of seeking out Hafiz to compliment him. Hafiz reported later: "The ambassador said that I should call upon him if I needed aid in continuing my education at the university. I replied that my

American friends had already been more than generous, but that I would visit his embassy before I returned to Pakistan."

"Did he make any inquiries about Saleem?"

"Only once. I said that Saleem had fallen ill in Chicago and sent his earnest regrets that he could not be present. The ambassador did not mention him again."

Some time the next day, Saleem returned from Chicago. Hafiz described him as being like a fighting cock who had lost half his comb and all his feathers. "He has been drunk for three days. His mind is so besotted that he did not know the ambassador had come and gone until I reminded him. He went into a fit of anger directed at me. Then he became much depressed."

At the end of the first semester, Saleem was put on probation because he had failed to take examinations. His college advisor informed him that he could enroll for the second semester but would be expected to make up the examinations he had missed and turn in all necessary term papers. Saleem immediately promised to reform and with Hafiz's constant tutoring showed some signs of recovery. After a few days, however, Saleem's resolution began to flag, and Hafiz had to devote so much time to his erratic countryman that his own work suffered. He was dismayed when he failed to receive his usual A's on two papers, and he informed me that he would have to drop some of his library hours in order to keep up with all the work he was doing for both himself and Saleem.

"Even though you do not share an apartment with Saleem," I reminded him, "he has made a servant of you."

Hafiz shook his head angrily. "He is like a spoiled child. Someone must look after him."

Late in the spring term, the dean of students called Saleem in and informed him that if there was not a marked improvement in his studies, he would be dropped from the college in June and could not be readmitted. From that day Saleem ceased attending classes, and though Hafiz certainly must have written papers for him, Saleem did not even bother to turn them in.

"Saleem is very sad," Hafiz told me one day, "very depressed and unhappy. I do what I can to comfort him, but he does not respond."

About two o'clock one morning my telephone rang me awake. It was Hafiz. Trying to keep his voice calm, he said, "Saleem just called my house. He was speaking like a hysterical girl. He first made me promise to arrange a Muslim funeral for him tomorrow, and then he said he was going to take an overdose of sleeping pills."

"Wake up the dean of foreign students," I said. "He'll know what to do."

"I have just tried to call him, sir. No reply. That is why I have called you." (I learned later that the dean of foreign students, after years of experience with late-night interruptions, always disconnected his telephone before going to bed.)

"Then give me Saleem's address," I said, "and I'll call an ambulance. I'll pick you up in about five minutes and we'll try to get over there by the time the ambulance arrives."

After calling the ambulance, I pulled a pair of trousers over my pajamas and ran for my car. Hafiz, fully dressed, was waiting on the sidewalk. We reached Saleem's apartment building a few seconds before the ambulance arrived with howling sirens and flashing lights. We all went in together. We found Saleem sprawled on his bed in his shorts, an empty bottle beside him. The hospital interns took over.

The report on Saleem was that he had taken only a small dose of sleeping pills, but next morning he was confined to a psychiatric ward and the dean of foreign students cabled his father in Pakistan. A few days later the old man arrived. After a series of stormy sessions with the dean of the college, the president of the university, and the director of the hospital (whose doctors stubbornly refused to release Saleem until all tests were completed), Saleem's father attached himself to Hafiz. When Hafiz came into the library to work, Saleem's father would come with him, seating himself at a study table and reading magazines. Then he would follow Hafiz out, going with him to classes, to the cafeteria, and even to the foreign students' house where Hafiz had found him a spare room. The old man wore a handsome gray beard that covered most of his chest, and he dressed in expensive silk suits. His fingers were covered with rings mounted with large precious stones.

"Saleem's father," Hafiz managed to inform me one morning,

"is trying to buy a master's degree for Saleem from the university. He talks to me about this constantly. He cannot understand why they will not take his money and issue the degree. He knows that he and his son will both lose face if they return to Pakistan without a degree. When I tell him that this is not the way things are done in America, he throws up his hands. He cannot understand. In Pakistan his wealth can buy anything. But not here. Not here."

A few days later, the hospital released Saleem, and he and his bearded, bejeweled father departed for Pakistan by way of Florida, where they had learned of a college from which degrees could indeed be purchased.

At last the incubus was off Hafiz's back. The day after he saw his countryman off, he came into the library smiling as though he had won a great victory. "Saleem will be happy with the master's degree his father is buying for him. In Pakistan no one will know that it is without value."

"You will know," I said.

"Yes, but I would never give him away."

"Too bad Saleem couldn't have been half the student you are."

Hafiz turned his head, staring across the library reading room into infinity. "He does not have the blood of an English lord in his veins."

"You and your English lord," I scoffed.

"Someone must be given the credit," Hafiz said very seriously.

As he progressed through the passing semesters toward his Ph.D., Hafiz won a series of honors, and always when I would compliment him, he passed off my remarks with some self-deprecating reply, ending up with a reference to the English lord.

In his final semester, his adviser belatedly and apologetically notified Hafiz that he had forgotten to inform him that a reading knowledge of German was a requirement for his doctorate degree. Instead of panicking, Hafiz calmly arranged for a tutor from the languages department and began a concentrated study of German. At the same time he continued writing his economics thesis. Thirty days later he passed the rather difficult examination which the professors of German prepared in those days, and he was declared proficient in the reading of that complicated language.

"Surely you must have had an undergraduate course," I said when I heard about this. "No one could pass a German reading test in so short a time."

"You forget," Hafiz reminded me, "that I'm the bastard son of an English lord."

"A German baron, more likely," I said, and Hafiz frowned severely at me. He never joked about that English lord.

As the day for graduation neared, Hafiz started worrying about his future after he returned to Pakistan. For the first time in months, he began referring to his low-caste birth. "No matter what employment I seek, they will not consider that I am a doctor of philosophy. They will say to themselves, 'This Dr. Hamid Hafiz, why he is only a Bhag-Nari nomad.' And then they will send me back to my camel."

Although he was armed with dozens of letters of commendation, Hafiz was still worrying on the day his small army of friends saw him off at the airport. Several days later, we began receiving occasional airmail letters postmarked from Karachi. Hafiz had been promised a small post in the Ministry of Agriculture ... He was still waiting ... He had obtained the position ... He had asked some of his new friends to seek out a marriageable girl of the caste above his ... He had looked at some photographs of the prospective girls ... He had arranged to see one of these girls, unobserved and unknown to her, as she walked along the street ... He was interested in this girl.

The letters stopped coming then, and after two or three months had passed without our hearing from Hafiz, a stranger walked into my library office one morning. "I promised Hamid Hafiz that I would not fail to bring you his special greetings when I came to the University of Illinois," he said.

The young man was a Quaker who had been on a study tour through India and Pakistan and was making a lecture circuit of campuses to report on his findings. During his travels in Pakistan, the Quaker had suffered an attack of dysentery so severe that he was forced to enter a Karachi hospital. He shared a room with a Pakistani who was ill with the same complaint. His roommate was Hamid Hafiz. "After four years in America," Hafiz ruefully explained to the Quaker, "I lost my immunity to our native microbes."

While they were convalescing, the two young men became good friends. Hafiz was feeling homesick for America, and the Quaker was delighted to find a Pakistani who knew what America was like. In spite of his illness, Hafiz was in high spirits because shortly after taking the government post he had received an appointment to teach economics in a small college. As soon as he was discharged from the hospital he was planning to go north to spend a few days with his family before reporting for his new duties.

Bit by bit, the Quaker learned about his roommate's nomadic origins, and one day he boldly asked if he might accompany Hafiz for the reunion with his people. At first Hafiz seemed reluctant, but when he came to realize that the American was genuinely interested, he consented.

In the heat of late summer, the two boarded a train that would take them up into northern Baluchistan. "The train was rickety, slow, crowded, and very uncomfortable," the Quaker told me. "But I enjoyed every moment of the journey. Along the way Hafiz remarked that his people had no conception of where he had been for the past four years. To them America was as remote as the moon, and his mother was convinced that devils had dragged him off to Hell."

"He was a remarkable student," I said, "to have come from a background of illiteracy and superstition, the first of his tribe to learn to read and write, and then go on to earn that Ph.D."

"He himself could not seem to understand how he had accomplished it," the Quaker said. "When the subject came up in our conversations, he would say something about having an English lord for a father."

"I know. I have heard all about that English lord."

The Quaker opened his briefcase. "Wait until you see the photographs I made of the homecoming." He began laying color snapshots out on my desk. The first one was made from a train window, a piece of scenery that might have been Arizona—arid desert land with dots of green vegetation fading off against an eroded ridge. The next was a ramshackle village, with forty or fifty people dressed in white kurtas and pajamas staring hard at the train.

The Quaker said, "I asked Hafiz if I might use my camera for the reunion. He said yes, except that I must not photograph the women. The train came to a stop and I followed Hafiz out to the vestibule. A grinning nomad in clean white dhoti leaped up on the step, barring our descent, motioning Hafiz to stand where he was. Outside, the men of the tribe were forming a double line for him to walk through. I took this shot hurriedly from the train." The photograph was slightly blurred, but the strong faces of the tribesmen were filled with a joyous pride. Even the graybeards were showing their teeth.

"I hurried to the next car exit," the Quaker said, "so that I could get some pictures of Hafiz coming down the line of honor."

These pictures, made out in the bright desert sunlight, were remarkably clear. One was of Hafiz stepping down from the old train, his head bowed to conceal his emotion. The next one showed him walking beneath the white-clothed arc of arms raised in a salute of honor, his dark head still bent forward. The last shot was a close-up of Hafiz's face as he came to the end of the honor guard and lifted his head.

"I'd never let Hafiz see this photograph," the Quaker said, "because there are tears in his eyes. He knew his people would think him unmanly if they saw the tears. He ruined my next shot by rubbing his sleeve quickly across his eyes."

There were dozens of other snapshots—of awestruck, half-naked boys gathered around Hafiz to admire him, of goat carcasses roasting over a pit, of dignified old men with white pugrees wound carelessly around their heads. "I wish I could have photographed Hafiz's mother, who bears some resemblance to him. Her face has great character, like that of a queen, and unlike most women of her age she seems quite young. Here is one of Hafiz with his father."

That was the most remarkable photograph of all, a head-and-shoulders portrait of father and son. They stood slightly apart, looking straight into the camera, the older man turbaned and dark-bearded, the younger man clean-shaven and wearing his bright orange necktie and the English lord's suit. Otherwise the two faces were mostly the same—noses slightly hooked, the moist brown eyes large and round and looking out at the world with mild astonishment and cynical amusement. As I studied the strangely familiar intelligent face of Hafiz's illiterate father, I was certain that the thought had never entered his mind that this brilliant young man being honored by the tribe that day might be the bastard son of an English lord.

CHAPTER THIRTEEN

Sleeping in Henry Shaw's Bed

LIKE MOST PEOPLE WHO EARN THEIR LIVINGS in our modern over-specialized civilization, librarians are occasionally called upon to be consultants. Librarians don't receive very much compensation for this work—if one can call it work—nothing like the sort of fees that engineers and computer experts command. Being summoned as a consultant, however, always makes a librarian feel important and offers a chance for him to travel somewhere at someone else's expense.

Once in a while a librarian becomes "typed" as a consultant, typed in a special field, I mean, and he may spend half his time traveling from one place to another offering sage advice. A number of years ago one of my friends in the library profession was chosen at random to make an honorary visitation to a new library in Africa, one of those new African countries. He knew very little about Africa, but as a result of that single journey he became known as a consultant on African libraries. As one African nation after another emerged from colonialism and felt the need for specialized advice on library development, my friend had to spend the remainder of his career jetting back and forth across the Atlantic. He hated airplanes, hated to fly, but there was no other African library consultant of his status, and he felt it his duty to keep going.

Nothing like this ever happened to me while I was a librarian. My field was overspecialized specialization in agricultural literature, and I can recall only three or four occasions when I was asked to be a consultant. The consultancy that I remember most vividly was when the Missouri Botanical Society invited me—in the late 1950s—to come to St. Louis to advise them on what to do about some problems in their library, and I wound up sleeping in Henry Shaw's bed.

The first I learned about this consultancy was from a colleague on the staff of the University of Illinois Library. His name was Harry Skallerup. He had been a student at Washington University in St. Louis and had taken some courses at the Missouri Botanical Society, or Shaw's Garden. The librarian there knew him quite well and had asked him to recommend an expert to advise them, and Harry out of the goodness of his heart recommended me. In turn, after I received a formal invitation by mail, I recommended that Harry accompany me to St. Louis as a collaborator.

Consequently, early one spring morning, filled with considerable self-importance, Harry and I set off across the Illinois prairies for St. Louis, to be consultants at the Missouri Botanical Society's library. To the people of St. Louis, the Society's headquarters is known as Shaw's Garden. It is an oasis set in the uplift of the city as it rolls westward from the Mississippi River. After driving through a red-brick jungle of urban decay, we came suddenly upon a towering limestone wall surrounding seventy-five acres of most extraordinary vegetation.

Shaw's garden then contained more than twelve thousand varieties of plants from all over the world, arranged into formal and informal gardens embellished with classical statuary or protected in greenhouses built unobtrusively into the backgrounds. An Englishman named Henry Shaw, who came to St. Louis early in the nineteenth century and made a fortune as a merchant, built a richly appointed house on the seventy-five acres and surrounded it with gardens worthy of the nobility of his native land. In 1858, Shaw endowed his estate as the Missouri Botanical Garden, and it has been thriving ever since.

Not long after Harry and I arrived at the gatehouse we were met by the librarian, Dr. George Van Shaack, who greeted us as though we were the possessors of some profound secret that would solve all his problems. He showed us where to park our car and escorted us into the gatehouse, a small building that was once used as a carriage house and living quarters for Henry Shaw's servants. The interior had been modernized into a suite similar to those of the best hotels and was used to house overnight guests of the botanical society. After depositing our luggage, we went with Van Shaack for a tour of his library.

Van Shaack was a dedicated botanist with a vast knowledge of the antiquarian books in his subject field, but he was quite baffled by the mass of current printed matter pouring into the society's library in a steadily increasing flood from similar institutions around the world. This, of course, is a problem faced by all libraries, especially those concerned with the sciences, and librarians who contend with this difficulty often go completely mad. They begin muttering about computers, data banks, and automated information retrieval; they call conferences and talk of hardware and software; they summon specialists from great corporations that manufacture business machines and other gadgets. Eventually these overly concerned librarians either end up working for one of the corporations they called in to help them or they are taken away to a rest home.

To avoid drowning in the print explosion of the sciences, librarians must float upon its billowing mass somewhat as surfers float upon great waves, balancing and compromising upon their surfboards and enjoying the exhilaration of being a part of this violent and unstable force that will carry us eventually, we hope, to some solid shore.

In the jargon of librarianship I conveyed these half-baked ideas of mine to Van Shaack, and although he may not have been impressed or reassured, he at least was generous enough to *pretend* that he was. After touring the library, which was spilling over with thousands of unbound and uncatalogued pieces of printed matter, we went to meet the director of the society. At that time the director was Edgar Anderson, a distinguished botanist with an international reputation for his work in hybridization. I soon discovered that Anderson was skeptical of my abilities to solve the library's problems, and I spared him the burden of advice I had given Van Shaack.

Later that afternoon Harry and I learned that the society had arranged for us to attend a dinner downtown where several members of the botanical staff would join us. Van Shaack explained that our dinner companions were carefully chosen *users* of the library who would want to raise questions during the evening. Because of a previous engagement, however, Edgar Anderson would not be able to join us.

The dinner was most enjoyable, with excellent wines to keep everyone in a congenial mood. If the botanists tossed any insoluble problems at their expert consultants from out of town I do not remember them.

When Van Shaack drove us back to Shaw's Garden about midnight, we found Edgar Anderson waiting for us in his car at the gatehouse. As we drove up, he got out and flagged us down. Resting on the gravel beside his car were two suitcases, mine and Harry's.

Anderson was in a grumpy mood. He began mumbling something about Sir John and Lady Smithton arriving a day early. "There was nothing else to do," he said to us, "but put Sir John and his lady in the gatehouse. As you can see, I brought out our library consultants' luggage."

Van Shaack gave Anderson a rather bleak look and then asked in a querulous voice: "Do you want me to drive our ejected guests to a motel?"

Anderson glanced at Harry and me. "Well," he said, "they *could* stay in Henry Shaw's house. It's up to them."

Van Shaack nodded. "It's never been done before, but I suppose the sheets and pillowcases are quite clean on Shaw's bed. And the motels are *miles* away from here."

About that time Harry spoke up politely: "It's all right with me. I don't mind sleeping in Henry Shaw's bed."

I agreed. Any bed good enough for Henry Shaw was good enough for me.

Anderson looked relieved. He turned toward his car. Harry and I picked up our suitcases. As we started off along a gravel path behind Van Shaack, Anderson called after us: "Be sure to warn them about tourists."

"Right," Van Shaack replied. In his calm way he began explaining who Sir John and Lady Smithton were. "Old friends of Edgar's," he said. "Sir John has done outstanding work on dwarf fruit trees and Edgar invited him over here to give a series of lectures. He was not supposed to arrive until tomorrow. It's too bad, putting you fellows out this way."

Both Harry and I insisted that we did not mind, although after the long day I was very much in need of a good bed and some restorative sleep, and I hoped Henry Shaw had possessed a good bed.

The spring night had turned muggy, and off to the west lightning was flickering. "We'll probably have a storm before morning," Van Shaack said. "Oh, by the way," he added, "the gates are opened at six A.M. for tourists. That early in the day visitors are usually garden club members passing through St. Louis who may have arrived too late the previous day for a visit. So we open at six o'clock in the morning as a courtesy to them. That way they can get an early start for wherever they may be driving. Garden clubbers are not likely to tour Henry Shaw's house, but some do. So you two had better be out of bed and dressed by six."

"That's awfully damned early," Harry said.

Van Shaack replied that he was sorry. By this time we had reached the rear entrance to Henry Shaw's mansion, a graceful two-story Italianate structure with an old-fashioned observation tower built on top of the roof. Van Shaack opened the door and switched on a dim bulb that barely illuminated a stairway. We followed him up the steps to a restraining rope strung between two solid pedestals in front of an open doorway. A sign hanging on the rope read: HENRY SHAW'S BEDROOM. NO ADMITTANCE. Van Shaack pushed one of the pedestals aside so that we could enter, and another low wattage bulb revealed a massive canopied bed.

Van Shaack went over and flung back the fancy gold coverlet, exposing two cased pillows and a sheeted mattress. "Looks very nice," he commented. "But I wouldn't use the chairs if I were you. They are more than a century old and the wood joints are probably very weak."

"We'll just get right into bed," I said.

Van Shaack nodded and turned to go. He said, "This house is never locked, but you're safer here than in a motel, with our high wall and iron gates between you and the city. Have a good night's sleep. But don't forget—up before six o'clock."

After he was gone, I tested the bed. Both the pillows and the mattress made a rustling noise under the slightest pressure. They were stuffed with excelsior or some sort of shredded wood. Harry was peering up at the massive canopy. "That canopy must weigh a ton," he said. "Made of heavy metal and something that seems to be imitation pearl."

"I hope it's structurally sound," I said. Feeling the burden of the day upon me, I got into my pajamas and literally fell into bed. It was like falling into a haystack. The mattress sagged slowly until my back pressed against wooden slats. Harry started to turn out the light. I suggested that he'd better put his watch in easy reach.

"I don't have a watch," he said. "I thought you had one."

I shook my head and asked, "How'll we know when it's six o'clock?"

"Oh, the birds'll wake us up," Harry said optimistically. With a crackling sound his body sank into the other half of the wooden-shavings mattress. Dust arose through the thin sheet and he began sneezing.

Sleep seemed impossible. If one of us moved, the rustling annoyed both of us. I tried lying on my back in motionless rigidity. Occasionally a flash of distant lightning revealed the menacing mass of heavy canopy suspended above us. Its shape and coloration reminded me of the interior of a giant oyster shell.

Some time or other I must have lost consciousness. A crash of thunder brought me out of a nightmare in which I was caught in the clasp of a giant oyster closing tight upon me. In an effort to escape the grip of the shell I jumped out of Henry Shaw's bed. Harry mumbled as he woke up: "What's the matter?"

"Nightmare," I said.

"This *is* a damned uncomfortable bed," he answered, and went back to sleep.

From a window I looked out at the rain-washed beauty of Shaw's Garden, which was illuminated by rapid flashes of spring lightning. After a while the thunderstorm died away. I lay down again upon my half of Henry Shaw's bed, and the steady drip of rain lulled me into a partial sleep.

Before morning I became enmeshed in another nightmare. Henry Shaw, a sturdy bearded man, had found me in his bed and was angrily trying to oust me from it by muscular force. In the irrationality of dreamland I tried to resist him instead of thanking him for removing me from his miserable bed. But actually it was only my friend Harry shaking me awake. Blinding sunlight was pouring through the high windows.

"Somebody's outside," Harry said. "Tourists, I think."

I rolled out and followed him to the window bay. Just below we could see the typical American family—father in a sport shirt looking bored and impatient, a boy and girl of the pre-teenage group, and a mother in a floppy wide-brimmed white hat. Mother was a Doris Day type of blonde; she was kneeling to peer into a flower bed.

"Garden clubbers," Harry said.

"How do you know?" I asked.

"The floppy white hat," he said. "All blonde garden club women wear floppy brimmed hats to keep from freckling."

As hastily as possible we got into our clothes, fastened our suitcases, and flung the coverlet back over the nonresilient mattress which still bore the deep imprints of our bodies. We scurried down the stairs and into a small washroom just in time to avoid meeting the Typical American Family who had decided to explore Henry Shaw's house. In a minute we could hear their voices and footsteps above us.

Harry was squinting at the dim lightbulb in the high ceiling above us. "No electric outlet anywhere," he said. "I suppose old Henry Shaw didn't own an electric razor. What kind of razor do you have?"

"Safety razor," I told him, "but there's no mirror, no hot water."

We decided to forgo shaving in favor of walking to a restaurant. We must have walked for miles, but found only a grocery store and had to settle for cold doughnuts and bananas for breakfast.

When we returned to Shaw's Garden, Dr. Van Shaack was waiting for us beside our car. He pretended not to notice our shabby overnight shadows of beards. "I hope you slept well," he said politely.

"Fine, fine," we both lied.

He asked, "Did you get up in time to miss the early tourists?"

"Just barely," I replied.

He smiled faintly and added, "I met a family just now who spoke admiringly of how well we keep up the Shaw house. The lady said the bedroom was most realistic, even to Shaw's yellow pajamas hanging from the canopy."

I felt like a fool. "I must have flung them up there while we were replacing the coverlet," I said. "I'll go get them."

He had my pajamas rolled up in a newspaper and thrust them upon me. He said, "I didn't disillusion the lady. But Henry Shaw surely must have worn a gray flannel nightshirt instead of yellow pajamas."

"Next time I come to be your library consultant," I said, "I'll bring a gray flannel nightshirt."

But there hasn't been any next time. Word must have got around. Since the night I slept in Henry Shaw's bed, nobody anywhere has ever asked me again to be a library consultant.

Notebooks, Best-sellers, and Serendipity

WRITERS ARE ASKED NUMEROUS QUESTIONS about writing. The questions come by mail and telephone, or from inquirers in person. What follows may answer some of these questions.

During and between the little adventures that I encountered while earning a living as a librarian, I tried always to keep a small notebook at hand. Except for the chapters of childhood and youth, almost everything written herein was first entered in rough form into a notebook. On occasions when a notebook was not in reach, I used the backs of letters, napkins, the margins of newspapers, or whatever scrap of paper was nearby.

Ideas, concepts, patterns—they can come from anywhere like flashes of lightning—and can vanish as swiftly unless they are put down on paper for future reference. Apt phrases, conjunctions of images in the mind, a human characterization can leap abruptly from one's surroundings, and a writer must seize upon these apparitions as gifts from Providence.

Notebooks are also useful for recording the essence of printed matter, or of words heard. A volume that may appear to be dull in its entirety to a casual reader may contain bright jewels for a writer, jewels for transfer into a notebook.

Had I not started a notebook of speeches made by American Indians of the nineteenth century I probably never would have written *Bury My Heart at Wounded Knee*. Long before the plan for that book was formed, I was collecting the poetic and symbolic words of American Indians wherever I encountered them. At first I had no intention of using them in a book, but collected them simply for what the words express—the human condition, love of the earth and its beings and the sky, devotion to a supreme power, heartbreaks and admonitions—spoken in rhythmic languages, at times lyrical, at times elegiacal.

Many of the better statements came from a most formidable collection of official documents known as the U.S. Serial Set, hundreds of volumes that stand little used in great libraries. Within this numbered series are official records of numerous meetings of government officials with representatives from Indian tribes, often called to discuss proposed treaties. Most of the Indian spokesmen used the languages of their tribes, and interpreters translated the words into English. In the latter half of the nineteenth century the government used Isaac Pitman's stenographic system to record and then start the translated words on their way to preservation in print.

Some of the speeches are so beautifully phrased that I was skeptical at first of the genuineness. Perhaps the translators were romantics, I thought, emulators of Wordsworth, Shelley, and Keats. I spent hours tracking down identities of the official interpreters, and eventually reached the conclusion that in most cases it mattered little who the interpreters were. The words came through into English with the same eloquence, seasoned with inspired metaphors and similes of the natural world.

Bury My Heart at Wounded Knee was a best-seller. I am not certain how or why this came about. Neither the publisher nor I expected the book to do little more than earn back its costs. Originally I intended it as a short volume for young readers, but after seeing the proposed outline my wise and long-suffering literary agent, Peter Matson, protested that this *must* be a book for all readers. The change of direction certainly added to its potential.

And then after *Bury My Heart* was published, Dick Cavett began quoting bits from it on his television show. At that time, Cavett had a nightly program on ABC that was of much higher quality than exists today on the networks. People who watched his show also read books. After a few weeks, he invited me to be a guest. The evening on which I appeared was also the evening of Hollywood's Academy Awards on another network, and he insisted that I return the following week. I am sure that Dick Cavett's interest in—and occasional warm comments about—the book had much to do with its success. Best of all, his enthusiasm was genuine. Although he projects the aura of an Easterner, Dick Cavett is a Westerner from

Caricature by Arkansas Gazette *cartoonist George Fisher*

Nebraska with a deep interest in frontier legend. After two decades we still communicate occasionally about various arcane pieces of Western America. Through the years Nebraskans have brought me good fortune—from McBrien, my professorial mentor, to Cavett, a scholar of the electronic age.

Perhaps it was timing, the attitude of the period, that had something to do with the popularity of *Bury My Heart*. It did seem to strike a response in the hearts of its readers, and more than twenty years later is kept in print in several languages.

Only two others of my books reached best-seller status, for short periods *Creek Mary's Blood*, a novel, and *The Gentle Tamers: Women of the Old West*. I do not know why they became best-sellers. No formula exists, that I know of, that will create a best-selling book.

In the process of preparing for and researching several of my books, serendipity has been surprisingly helpful in guiding me to the exact information I needed, or into unknown pathways that proved beneficial for me to follow. On numerous occasions, I would be searching in one direction in vain when suddenly serendipity would make an appearance and lead me directly to an unexpected but ideal solution that I was totally unaware of.

The origin of the word *serendipity* is an enchanting story in itself. It comes from a Persian fairy tale concerning three princes of Serendip (the ancient name for present day Sri Lanka). Throughout the tale, the three princes are continually making marvelous discoveries while looking for something else.

One of the oft-told examples of serendipity is Alexander Fleming's providential discovery of penicillin. He was conducting routine experiments when an accidental laboratory spill led to penicillin. However, had Fleming not been a thorough student of bacteriology and a keen observer, serendipity might have led him blindly past the presence of penicillin. Like Fleming, writers must have the skill and power of observation to recognize what serendipity is trying to do for them.

I believe that each human being has within himself or herself at least one poem or short story, or perhaps a full-length book. Practice, practice, and a few nudges from serendipity are the generating forces.

So let us become serendipists and keep in mind this paraphrased wisdom from Thomas Carlyle: The art of writing is the most miraculous of all things man has devised.